The New Testament
as the
Church's Book

The New Testament as the Church's Book

by WILLI MARXSEN

translated by JAMES E. MIGNARD

FORTRESS PRESS

Philadelphia

Contents

Introduction

THE OCCASION

This book is deliberately polemical. In a controversy there are two ways to proceed. One may choose to attack the opposition *directly* by setting forth its views, pointing out its contradictions, shortcomings, and invalid conclusions, thereby refuting it. Or one may attack *indirectly* by firmly establishing his own position, particularly with regard to debatable points. Opposing ideas then appear as another possibility, yet are defeated, and one's own arguments are examined at the same time. I have chosen the second way.

In order to gain some perspective of the issues covered in this book, a few preliminary remarks on the theological and ecclesiastical situation are necessary. Our theme is "The New Testament as the Church's Book." At the end of the title there is a period, implying that an affirmation is being made. One may conceivably object that my affirmation is so obvious and so indisputable it needs no discussion. Not even the person who has washed his hands of the church will challenge it; in fact, even though he is outside of the church, he will still be in a position to determine that the New Testament is the church's book, provided, of course, he is given enough

1

information. Therefore, am I not simply belaboring the obvious when I say the theme implies an affirmation? Not at all!

Certain groups within the Protestant church in recent years have frequently raised the cry publicly that modern theology, and in particular, modern exegesis, have not accorded the New Testament the respect to which it is entitled as the church's book. The manner in which the New Testament is treated by modern, scientific theology and by historico-critical exegesis demonstrates that it is no longer the church's book, because it is no longer a book *sui generis* (constituting a class by itself). Men look upon it as they do any other popular literary work; its high position is diminished, and it is studied and interpreted by the same basic methods that are applied to other literature. In short, the New Testament becomes a work of secular literature instead of remaining the church's book.

If all this were true, a "modern" theologian would indeed no longer have the right to place a period after our theme; a question mark would be much more appropriate. My dispute is in fact with this question mark although I do not intend to attack it. I plan rather to emphasize the period so strongly that, when we are finished, an exclamation point will in fact be required. The real debate, therefore, is whether a period or a question mark should be used, and when I insist upon a period, I begin the controversy.

I want to make the outlines of our theme somewhat clearer by speaking in a less technical way for the moment and filling in some details of the problem. Let me begin with the admission that I can fully understand why "the other side" would complain that modern theology ought to place a question mark after the title. It is clear to me why the idea has come about that due to modern theology the New Testament loses its character as a book *sui generis* and with this loss its character as the church's book. I will comment on this briefly and perhaps will touch upon experiences that some readers have had.

Many of you come from church-related circles such as youth groups or the YMCA where you attended Bible studies or even conducted them yourselves. Through these studies or your private reading of the Bible you developed a certain relationship to the Bible. Later, you decided to study religion (as a major or minor) at college, or you occasionally attended lectures on religion at college to see how the knowledge you gained in the church fared in academic halls. To your surprise you discovered that the attitude toward the Bible there was entirely different from what you had grown used to. You heard, for example, that this or that was a myth and therefore not to be understood historically, or that it was not possible (historically) to know very much about Jesus. You were told that Jesus was not born in Bethlehem, as you had learned from the Christmas story, but (as far as it can be determined at all) in Nazareth. You may also have been told that it is necessary to examine the contents of the New Testament before judging whether they are true, even theologically true.

In other words you met what is usually called "biblical criticism" and you could easily have gained the impression that men with their reason were trying to set themselves up as judges over the Bible. But do they have such a right? Would this not destroy the very basis of faith? Should not the critic also stand mute before the Bible? What is really the correct approach to the Bible— the one you had previously used or the one now being shown you? You may have already asked yourself this last question, and if so, you are reflecting the scholarly attitude which inquires after truth without insisting that the truth has always been in its possession and which recognizes, at the same time, that the disclosure of truth is not infrequently preceded by painful experiences (often affecting one's personal life).

Much of what was discussed in the lecture halls and seminars reached the outside. Whether this was always done tactfully is a question that need not be answered here, but it is understandable that it unsettled the churches and caused unrest. The less the churches were informed, the more their uneasiness increased. Regardless of the direction the conflict took, an actual discussion of the issues never developed. Instead, incautious warnings against heresy were flung out on a large scale and sweeping judgments made which revealed both a frightening lack of understanding of the problem and a great lack of love. Open letters were written and petitions submitted to church authorities demanding that steps be taken to correct a situation in which university professors dared to present such views. Because they were destroying the faith, the professors were asked to resign. A letter of January 1, 1961 with fifty signatures to the administration of the *Evangelische*

Landeskirche in Württemberg reads: " . . . it is an intolerable contradiction to call for empowered witnesses of the Gospel in the church when they will be educated in places where the very basis of faith *may be systematically destroyed*."

May be systematically (!) destroyed. As a result of these harsh words and similar statements I can understand why one theological faculty refused to discuss the open letter. It was assumed by the professors that this kind of accusation was proof that any true basis for mutual discussion no longer existed. According to the usual vocabulary of these groups systematic destruction of the basis of faith means systematic destruction of the Bible as the church's book or systematic secularization of the Bible. We ought, for a moment, to think about what is being said here. The complaint is not that the professors are indifferent to matters of faith, or that they are not regular churchgoers, or anything of the sort. Rather, they are being accused of deliberately destroying the very reasons which lead their students to study theology in the first place. And in the face of such a charge it is quite legitimate to ask whether there is indeed any basis for mutual discussion. I, for one, however, do not want to break off the conversation and in spite of these allegations I am going to place a period—even an exclamation point—after the title. It should be clear by now, I think, that the problem really concerns the use of a period or a question mark.

One matter cannot pass unmentioned, namely, denouncing opponents for heresy without first thoroughly and competently refuting them. Church history furnishes evidence that this has not always been true of Christians. But even though we may learn from the past, the history of the church cannot excuse such actions today. We ought to try, then, to know each other better, since each stands under the judgment of the other. I want both parties to hear this and I hope, thereby, to strike at the root of an extremely bitter attitude.

I shall begin with us, the ones who are attacked. Modern theology certainly cannot do itself harm by frankly recognizing that the indictments against it are brought by groups in which a very active church life is usually found. This of course does not justify their theological views since the success of an idea does not mean it is correct, nor is a correct idea guaranteed success (this is just as true in the secular realm). So, a vital church life is no criterion for the correctness of their position. The people of Corinth who fell away from Paul (and from his Gospel) were extraordinarily active in the church and possessed a flourishing personal life. But neither this nor his own—temporary, at least— failure ruffled Paul. Nevertheless, we should realize that the attack on modern theology is launched from just such thriving churches.

On the other hand, it will not hurt the accusing factions to learn that modern theology is concerned with intellectual honesty, even in matters of faith. This admission does not imply that faith is at the mercy of the *ratio*, the intellect, but if faith is to make a total claim upon an individual, the claim must include the intellect; this area of a believer's life cannot be excluded. In practice, however, is not the intellect actually pushed aside when it is emphasized that "reason" should allow itself to be taken captive? This sounds rather strange. To understand what is meant, some distinction between "reason" and "intellect" may be helpful. The former may be defined as man's capacity to perceive and the latter as his ability to evaluate and work out the implications of what he has perceived. But when the revelation of God comes upon a believer, he must respond to it even though he is a person capable of reasoning. Yet, he is not asked to surrender his rational faculties! We do not expect the churchgoer to check his intellect with the sexton before entering the church and then to pick it up when he leaves because it will be needed later on the outside! Does he take along an intellect unaffected by the Christian message? To keep the intellect apart from faith is nothing less than a declaration that there is an area of life which has nothing to do with faith. It is curious how the representatives of this attitude adroitly make use of the intellect in the detailed defense of their ideas, and in view of this I think they should stop slighting or condemning the efforts of modern theology to preserve intellectual honesty. The accusation that the intellect has assumed priority over faith is malicious, for even though it may occasionally be true, one should not conclude that such shortcomings in the theological enterprise are part of a deliberate program.

These two points—active church life in the one group and intellectual honesty in the other—are the areas each sees as lacking in the other. A realistic acknowledgment of these differences would reveal to each side its own inadequacies and could lead to a renewed concern for their common task. Modern theologians, for example, could ask themselves (more than they have in the past): "How can the results of our studies offer help in specific areas to the church (which is dependent upon leadership and guidance) so that it is *strengthened,* and our research does not remain merely the intellectual property of a few scholars?" Church groups could also consider their obligation in reaching modern man who is not prepared to—indeed, cannot and may not—perform a *sacrificium intellectus* (sacrifice of the intellect) when he believes, and who cannot live a naive, simple life in the church while outside of the church taxing all his resources in a struggle for survival in business and in his daily routine. I have set these problems before you candidly because I want you to know the background of what will be covered in this book.

THE PROBLEM

I have said that a period and not a question mark belongs after the title. The period is polemical insofar as it implies a denial of the charge that modern theology (or modern exegesis) makes it impossible to think of the New Testament as the church's book, and, thus, as a special book. One particular matter should be discussed here. It will not do to insist that a document is authoritative if no instructions are given on how it is to be used or interpreted. In preambles to church constitutions or regulations, for example, there is usually a declaration to the effect that the church is founded upon the witness of the prophets and apostles of the Old and New Testaments, and this is generally followed by appropriately selected articles of faith. The basic role of the Old and New Testaments here is not disputed, but the bare statement leaves too much unsaid. In what way is an authoritative word derived from these writings? Should we interpret the Old Testament, for example, spiritually, typologically, or allegorically? Should we interpret it in a historico-critical manner, or should we approach it—and this is quite possible—uncritically and simply understand it as a historical account? In each case the document remains the same, but by itself says nothing; only through the act of interpreting is it made to say anything. However, different methods of interpretation yield widely disparate results, so that determining the correct method for the church is of fundamental importance!

The traditional preambles to church constitutions, therefore, gloss over a problem that needs to be resolved if they are ever to be of any practical use. They ought, for example, to say something like this: The church is founded upon the witness of the Old and New Testaments as this is interpreted by the historico-critical method (or any other method, for that matter). The only point I want to make here is that as long as the method of interpretation is not specified, an appeal to the Old or New Testaments is meaningless, since I can prove from the Bible whatever I want if I am allowed to choose how I am going to interpret it. Let me repeat: These preambles overlook a problem that must be resolved before they can ever be useful. Only a person who feels at home in the darkness can be satisfied with statements like these that really say nothing.

This brings us back to the question mark. Modern exegesis looks as much to the Bible as the traditional exegesis of the church ever did. In the great majority of examples of schism in the church, both sides have rested their cases on the Bible. But the Bible has always remained the same (apart from the difference raised by the so-called Apocrypha, which is recognized by Rome, rejected by Geneva, and left undecided by Wittenberg). Yet, even though it has never changed, such diverse teachings have been derived from it that at times men have despaired of preserving the unity of the church. Strictly speaking, then, the issue is not whether modern theology *permits* the Bible to be used as the church's book, but, in view of the methods employed by modern theology, whether it can still be *used* as the church's book. It would be an error, or at least a gross simplification, to insist that the conflict is with the Bible itself. The struggle focuses on the correct use that is to be made in applying it to the church's life. The object (the Bible) cannot be separated here from the way it is used (the method), and since the text always remains the same, the problem is fundamentally one of methodology. I want to emphasize, however, that methods of interpretation should not be developed apart from the Bible itself.

These introductory remarks suggest the direction the discussion in this book should take. Let me express this by referring again to the punctuation marks. The purpose of the first chapter of the book is to show how the idea of a question mark arose. In the second chapter it is to examine the degree of justification for the question mark (as opposed to an uncritical period). And, finally, in the third chapter we will examine how defensible a period is in spite of the question mark. I am quite aware that this is only a rough sketch which still needs to be filled in.

When I announced this series of theological lectures for all students of the university, I was aware of an obligation. I determined to take pains to explain the problems as clearly as possible and to avoid the technical language of theology as much as possible, or else make the terms intelligible. This is because I had in mind the theologian's responsibility to point out to the non-theologian the significance of theological scholarship for faith. For if it is true (and it very likely is) that because of modern exegesis the non-theologian no longer knows what his relationship is to the New Testament or the Bible as a whole or how he is to use it, it becomes the task of the theologian to show him. And it is just this that I want to try to do.

1.

The New Testament
as the
Work of the Church

To call the New Testament the church's book is to describe it as the book from which the church lives. In a sense the Old Testament should also be considered here, but I am excluding it, even though in the Introduction I frequently spoke of the Bible as the book from which the church lives. I am doing this for practical reasons only and not because I want to pronounce judgment on the Old Testament, nor because the Old Testament problems at this point are especially difficult—they are, as a matter of fact, more difficult than those of the New Testament as modern Old Testament studies show, although this apparently has not yet been recognized in the church. But its omission here is justified because in a special sense the New Testament is more the church's book than the Old Testament, a point everyone will accept.

The New Testament as the church's book is thus the book from which the church sustains its life, as it finds there its source for preaching, doctrine, order, and teaching. Its use, however, is not restricted to these areas, for the church also encourages its members to use it for their personal growth. A brief survey like this may leave the impression that members of the church study this book passively rather than critically because it is their authority or "canon," their guide to follow. In the sixteenth century the church was reformed when it turned to it, and even today teaching and preaching are considered valid only if they have biblical support. The church rejects every attempt to introduce any other authority, whether it is tradition, society, a people and their history, or even national pride.

Why, then, did the idea ever arise in the first place that a question mark should follow our theme so that we need to consider it now? The reason is that this apparently simple expression—the book from which the church lives—conceals problems which raise a host of difficult questions as soon as their nature is understood. The New Testament has not always been the norm for the church. The unqualified statement that the New Testament is the book from which the church lives is therefore incomplete. It is more accurate to say that beginning at a definite time it became the book from which the church lived. But what of the church before that time? And what is the relationship between the church that had not yet begun to derive spiritual life from the New Testament and the church that afterwards did? What, in other words, can we say about the continuity of the church? Before answers to these and related questions can be suggested, certain facts need to be firmly established.

THE LIMITS OF THE NEW TESTAMENT

For a considerable time the ancient church was not at all certain which of the earliest Christian writings should be recognized as canonical; in fact, the matter was often the subject of vigorous debate. The oldest list of canonical writings we have, the so-called Muratorian Canon of the second century (after Muratori, a librarian in Milan who published the fragment in 1740), bears witness to the uncertainty. This document is the remainder of a list (in barbarous Latin) from which not only several writings are omitted that are found in the New Testament today (the Letter of James and the Letter of Peter, for example), but in which several are mentioned that are not included in our present canon (the Wisdom of Solomon, for example, which is usually considered a part of the Old Testament Apocrypha, and the Revelation of Peter). Furthermore, it contains statements that indicate that the limits of the canon had not yet been firmly established. The acceptance of the Revelation of Peter, for instance, met with opposition: "Also of the Revelations we accept only those of John and Peter, which [i.e. the Revelation of Peter] some of our people do not want to have read in the churches." There is also a report of the difficulty another writing, the *Shepherd of Hermas*, had in its bid for recognition because of its late date.

A large number of additional witnesses, apart from the Muratorian Canon, also testify to indecision over the canonicity of certain writings at that time. On the other hand, several documents which were eventually not considered canonical were held in high esteem, e.g., the

Gospel of the Hebrews, the Gospel of the Egyptians, the Didache (the Teaching of the Twelve Apostles), 1 Clement (written in A.D. 97 by a Roman elder to the church in Corinth), and others.

For our study it is important to notice that the church was not able to achieve unanimity in these matters. Decisions on the writings varied from one church district to another as spirited discussions took place to decide which of them should possess canonical validity, and therefore, authority, and which should not. We need not develop this aspect of the problem any further as long as we are aware that the canon—or, the developing canon—was the subject of lengthy theological discussions. Unfortunately, these discussions also were occasions for charges of heresy which were hurled against representatives of opposing views.

The disagreement over the canon was tentatively resolved around the end of the fourth century when its perimeter was defined as we know it today. In the East this was accomplished through the Thirty-Ninth Festal Letter of Athanasius of Alexandria in A.D. 367 and in the West in A.D. 382 by the synod of Rome, joined later by North African synods. Nevertheless, the controversy over some writings persisted despite both Athanasius's Letter and the decision of the synod of Rome. Some of the codices of the Bible and of the New Testament from the fourth century and later, for example, included works that were not found on the lists of Athanasius or of the synod of Rome.

We may infer from all this that the canon (better, the limits of the canon) of the New Testament was the work

of the church which decided for itself what should be
authoritative.

The Significance of the Ancient
Church's Decision

This last statement which is historically tenable is not
seriously challenged today, but it does pose one question. If the church itself was responsible for deciding
which writings were to act as its norm, what then
actually was that norm? The writings? Or, more plau-
sibly, the church itself, since it was here that the norm
was defined? Only one aspect of the question needs to be
taken up here. The Protestant church, born in the
Reformation, maintains that its norm is the Bible alone:
sola scriptura. This position, however, requires some
understanding of the church's role in the origins of the
canon, especially since the church did not become active
in the process in the first century, but in the fourth, a
relatively late date. The Protestant then faces the
dilemma that the canon could not have served as a
guideline as the church debated the problem, since the
canon did not yet exist! In other words, the church was
not able to abide by the principle *sola scriptura* in
deciding what should or should not be canonical. At the
time canonical Scriptures were unknown, and the
church's decision could in no way be "according to
the Scripture."

Occasionally the position is taken that it was not
really the church which determined or defined the
canon. Instead of constituting the canon by an authoritative pronouncement, so the argument goes, it simply
declared those writings to be canonical that had already

proven themselves to be canonical through long use. Christians had always consulted a number of different writings, but around the fourth century they began to ask themselves what they, at least, should accept as an authoritative guide. They were looking, of course, to works already in existence and after weighing the attitudes of other Christians toward the different writings declared what was in fact canonical.

This certainly was a factor in the history of the canon, and insofar as it is a true description of what happened, it prevents the church's decision from appearing as compulsive or arbitrary. But a problem still remains, for the solution makes the experiences of men the standard for what should be (or better, should remain) canonical. Experiences, however, can be deceitful allies in such decisions, and it is fair to ask whether the experiences of one individual are binding on another. It is by no means theoretical, therefore, to suggest that the ancient decision on the canon made on the basis of fourth century experiences is open to revision. Luther, for example, held a negative attitude toward the Letter of James calling it a strawy epistle and placed it last in the canon. He has frequently drawn fire for this today even from Protestant theologians. But the basic question still remains. Why shouldn't the modern church have the same right of making its experiences normative as the fourth century church? Or were those fourth century experiences in some way special?

The Canon and Faith

From time to time the claim is made that the canon should be treated as an object of faith, although it is beyond me how anyone can propose this. Faith is said to be involved in that we are faced with a decision of faith by the church and are to exercise our faith by consenting to that ancient decision. Acceptance of the canon then becomes a matter of faith. This looks like an easy solution, but it is vulnerable for the simple reason that the canon did not fall from heaven all at once as an entity to be believed in. One cannot emphasize too much that the canon was a part of the fabric of church history. But if it developed within history what are we then supposed to put our faith in? When the problem is studied more closely, it becomes evident that the canon is not an object of faith (it is not clear, anyway, what this really means) to be believed. What does become evident is that some Christians believe that the decision on the canon made so long ago was correct, that at the time it was quite possible to make a correct decision of this type which we are to accept, and that the church was guided by the Holy Spirit in such a way that it was able to decide correctly (and with finality). Those who speak of the canon as an object of faith are not arguing about the canon (whether they know it or not); they really mean that they trust and participate in a decision of the church.

The implication of this position should be drawn out. Anyone who insists that the church (led by the Holy Spirit) was able to decide on the structure of the canon will hardly admit that the Spirit left the church as soon as the decision was cast; it is not clear to me, at least, how such an idea could be defended. But if the Spirit did not abandon the church, why shouldn't the church at a later date be able to make similar decisions? Such decisions could not, of course, be shown to be the result of the Spirit's guidance. The Spirit is not a *methodological* principle whose working is subject to detailed analysis. But when one introduces the Spirit into the argument he should be consistent and not arbitrarily allow the Spirit a role in the church's decisions at one season and then deny it the same role at a later date. Protestant theology is sometimes myopic in this regard. It agrees that the canon arose under the supervision of the Spirit, but the unavoidable consequence of this view is that the norm for the church for all time is no longer the New Testament but the Holy Spirit who guided the church. However, since the Spirit's work cannot be shown to be the work of the Spirit, faith must be focused on the church as the vehicle of the Spirit, and this means the church would be her own norm.

These are the only choices: Either the decision of the fourth century is subject to revision, thereby rendering all of the church's decisions liable to revision, or tradition (as it is commonly understood) becomes the norm. The Roman Catholic church has adopted the latter position which, in its implications, is by far the more consistent. We should not overlook this. By now it should be apparent that the view the Protestants have held since the Reformation is no true alternative. They claim to recognize only the principle *sola scriptura* (the canonical Scriptures alone), while the Catholics appeal to both "Scripture and tradition," but the Protestant position does not really offer a genuine alternative, for whoever adopts the principle of *sola scriptura* rests his case upon the New Testament of Athanasius and the synod of Rome; that is, he also depends upon tradition, the decision of the church. If Protestants ask that an exception be made in this one instance, they must still justify such an arbitrary request, and it is doubtful that they can. They will succeed, I am afraid, only if they are willing to put up with additional inconsistencies. In the choice of either "the Scriptures only" or "Scripture and tradition" the Roman Catholic church easily has the better position; for (this I say very pointedly) whoever takes as his only norm the New Testament within its canonical limits travels the road of the Roman Catholics, except that he is less consistent than they.

"The New Testament as the church's book" is, therefore, not only "the book from which the church lives." It is also "the book whose limits have been defined by the church" and this means that the canon does not exist independently of the ancient church. At best, it is the modern church that has an independent existence— vis-à-vis a fourth century decision.

Revision of the Canon

The critical problems could be dismissed simply by insisting that the process of canonization which was completed by ecclesiastical decision is subject to basic revision. Otherwise, tradition would become the norm. This suggestion, however, is not very practical and is frequently the product of anti-Catholicism (that is, tradition may not be the norm), a poor basis for scholarly judgments on controversial issues. Why cannot tradition be normative? If neither the canon in its present form may be the norm (since it may be revised) nor tradition, what can be? I will deal with this shortly but first I want to reject as unrealistic the notion that we must consider the canon open to revision to prevent tradition from becoming the norm. This view has never been of any practical consequence anyway. Occasionally one hears that the borders of the canon are still fluid, but this usually appears to be more hypothetical than serious, and, as far as I know, up to now no one has ever successfully followed through on it. Even today, for example, Luther's attitude toward the Letter of James has its critics. And whenever the remark is made that the limits of the canon are not fixed, it is often followed in the same breath by the statement that the canon of the ancient church is, nevertheless, still to be retained.

The view just outlined could be defended in order to cripple discussion of this difficult problem. If we determine that this should not happen, it implies a judgment of our own with regard to that view. The subject of the revision of the canon is of profound significance. To say that it *may* be revised is not the same as saying it *must* be. That it must not be, as some contend, is again the result of a personal judgment and immediately brings up the matter of criteria and their sources which support such an attitude. It is appropriate here to look at this more closely and inquire about the criteria for canonicity the ancient church used.

The Norm

We have been trying to avoid the conclusion that the church—both ancient and modern—is its own norm. It is not our right, however, to state *de novo* what should and should not be canonical, because we would ourselves then be establishing the norm. Of more importance to us is the search for criteria lying outside the church (ancient and modern). If we are able to locate such criteria—for the ancient as well as for the modern church —we will possess the possibility of checking both the decision of the fourth century and ours today.

It will be helpful to turn to the historical context again. I said that the emergence of the canon culminated in a declarative pronouncement and that the experiences of the church with the writings played a role in this. Experiences, however, could hardly have been the norm since not only are a variety of experiences possible, but in the early church there were differing experiences with different documents in different church areas. When agreement was being reached on the present limits of the canon, there was no appeal to or comparison of experiences. The church looked instead to definite criteria open to examination.

In the Muratorian Canon one finds the belief that canonicity is related to the age of writings. The *Shepherd of Hermas* is rejected because it was written "quite lately in our own time in the city of Rome, when on the throne of the church of the city of Rome the bishop Pius, his brother, was seated." According to the lists of Roman bishops this was around the middle of the second century. The interesting point here is that whatever came into being "in our time" could not be canonical, implying that no one would presume to write anything claiming apostolic validity. The basic principle, apparently, was that a writing could be considered canonical only if it was apostolic; that is, canonical authority was not to be attributed to a writing unless it came from the apostles and their disciples. For this reason a writing not dated before the second century could not be canonical because it was not apostolic. For the moment we can delay taking up the question of whether equating "apostolic" with "canonical" is justified. We have at hand a criterion that may be examined, and it is of more immediate interest to us to see how it was used.

A quick look into the New Testament confirms that the principle was consistently applied, at least as far as the present titles of the individual books are concerned. Matthew and John belong to the twelve, while Mark and Luke are "disciples of the apostles." The letters of Paul are apostolic, Peter is an apostle, and Jude and James, as brothers of Jesus, belong to the same circle. Thus according to the names ascribed to each book, the entire New Testament is included with the exception of the Letter to the Hebrews, which the ancient church nevertheless assumed was by Paul.

The problem of authorship, however, was thornier than may appear, for in the ancient church the authorship of many writings was disputed—this is not a fiction of the modern critic! Origen in the third century, for example, argued against the "genuineness" of the Letter of James, denying that it was written by the brother of the Lord. And Eusebius in the fourth century recorded that the Revelation of John was supposed to have come not from the apostle John, but from an elder named John. A considerable number of writings can be cited whose apostolic authorship was doubted by the ancient church and which, accordingly, were not admitted to the canon because they were adjudged "not genuine." The concept of "not genuine" is in itself open to question, but has nevertheless become the accepted term. It merely says that a writing is not by the one whose name is given as the author; in other words, not genuine simply means "pseudonymous."

We should not suppose that the men of the ancient church engaged in historical research for enlightenment on the question of authorship, since historical research, at least as we know it today, was unknown. The general rule rather was to use the contents of the writings as the basis for "historical" judgments on authorship, although this led them to move in a circle. They reasoned that a writing could and should be canonical only if it was apostolic; if its apostolicity was uncertain, the contents were examined to see if there was agreement with what they themselves considered to be canonical. The church-men assumed this right because they believed that as heirs of the true apostolic tradition they were in possession of the true teaching. Today the methods of research are more rigorous and frequently lead to different (historical) conclusions on authorship. The point I am stressing is that authorship was of fundamental concern to the ancient church, since confident knowledge here made it possible to determine what was apostolic and, therefore, what was to be valued as canonical. As a consequence, later writings, even though they contained "true apostolic" teaching, were not admitted to the canon. On the other hand, the Letter to the Hebrews was brought into the canon not because there were no objections to its contents, but because of the conviction that it had been written by Paul.

Before we inquire whether this criterion—canonical = apostolic—is justified, I should like to pose one question with regard to the last paragraph. What would happen if we today could show that the historical decisions of the ancient church on the authorship of several writings were incorrect? Scarcely any modern New Testament scholar assumes that Paul wrote the Letter to the Hebrews or that Peter wrote 2 Peter, for example. In both cases there is almost complete agreement not only among Protestant scholars who specialize in such study, but among Roman Catholic scholars as well. If the ancient church had come to the same conclusions, it is very likely that it would not have included these two letters in the canon. And if we could have the advice of the ancient church about what action we should take today, we would be told to remove both writings from the canon. To dispute this would be to accuse the ancient church of not taking its own criteria seriously, and this we have no right to do!

An overall view of our problem shows that it is contrary to the facts to regard the canon as though it had been given all at once in its final form, since the decisions on its limits were based on historical judgments. But a historical judgment, such as a verdict on authorship, is itself always subject to a thoroughgoing examination and is not something one decrees. If better methods for historical study are available to us today (as is true in the two examples cited above), it makes it impossible for us to do nothing and simply rest content with the bare statement that the limits of the canon may be redefined. It is just when we treat the criteria of the ancient church seriously that we come face-to-face with the demand—not merely the permission—to apply them once again to determine what is canonical. And when we do, we find that we must exclude Hebrews and 2 Peter, at least, from the canon.

Is the Decision of the Ancient Church Final?

A common objection to what I have just said is that we are studying historical problems—nothing more—and we have no right to make theological assessments from historical data on something like apostolic authorship. Even if the Letter to the Hebrews is not from Paul or 2 Peter from Peter, this has nothing to do with the contents which may still be true! I do not want to discuss this except to remark that if this line of reasoning is valid, I can point to other writings from that period (and even later) whose contents are also theologically correct. But then it would not be clear to me why the preference for Hebrews and 2 Peter was so strong that they were admitted to (or left in) the canon while others were not. Hebrews and 2 Peter cannot be "saved" for the canon merely by pleading that their contents are free of objections, for I would then have to accept as canonical all other writings whose contents are not objectionable. We can only conclude that if it is correct to equate "canonical" with "apostolic," both of these writings will have to be removed from the canon.

Occasionally there is an attempt to circumvent these difficulties by asserting that the canon arose *confusione hominum* but *providentia Dei*, that is, through human confusion but in accordance with divine providence. This is an extremely weak argument here, although I do not deny that things like this happen. That God can still bring blessings out of human errors is a miracle we are aware of all too often. But we certainly cannot apply this principle to the canon and insist that God made use of the historical errors of the ancient church to produce the blessings of the canon! The most we can say is that it

was the providence of God that the church was not ship-
wrecked on a canon which, according to the church's
own criteria, was incorrectly determined! This does not
of course justify once and for all the existence of an
obvious error, and I am puzzled why such faulty thinking is so prevalent. If blessings result in spite of or even
through an offense of mine, the offense is still an offense,
and I have no right to conclude that I may repeat it since
it will produce blessings again! If no harm comes from a
human error, there are still no grounds for justifying it, if
it is recognized as error in the first place.

In summary we may say this: The ancient church
wanted to canonize what was apostolic, but in the
process error slipped in. If we intend to remain obedient
to the ancient church—for whatever the reasons may be—
we have to accept its criteria but not its conclusions,
since in several places they have turned out to be incorrect. For this reason the limits of the canon as set by the
ancient church remain in question.

The Theological Question

The church itself was responsible for defining the
limits of the canon. The apparent danger in this seems
to be that when it did so, it produced its own norm, and
instead of having a truly external reference point, it had
only its own decision as a gauge. In the course of our
study we have seen that this was not actually the case.
The church did indeed mark out an external reference
point by means of a declarative act, but in doing so used
a criterion that was external to itself, viz., canonical =
apostolic. Accordingly, the "canon" of the canon of the
New Testament is apostolic authorship, and it is this

"canon" that provides the criterion for examining the canon of Scripture.

An obvious question here is whether this "canon" (canonical = apostolic) is really proper. In using the concept "canon" I am differentiating between the canon of Scripture (the usual meaning) and the "canon" of the canon of Scripture, the latter to be understood as the criterion (or the norm) by which the canon of Scripture is to be tested. This will be important for a later discussion.

We have seen that such a distinction is necessary in considering the historical data associated with the ancient church. It is reasonable to inquire now whether this newly discovered "canon" is appropriate. At this point we only know that the ancient church made use of it. It could well be that the church itself thought it up. If that were true, the setting of the limits of the canon of Scripture would have been accomplished by a declaration of the ancient church, but the determination of the criterion used in setting these limits would have been a constitutive act of the church itself. And then we would have made little headway toward a solution and a spate of problems would still remain. Hence an answer is required to the question of whether it is acceptable to equate "apostolic" with "canonical."

Summary: We have been asking about the limits of the New Testament and have seen that the criterion employed in setting those limits can be examined. The criterion, in turn, introduces a new criterion, and this means that the New Testament is not the church's norm as though it were given in final form all at once, but is the norm only as it relies upon the "canon" we have described as "canonical=apostolic." The norm for the church, therefore, is not the New Testament but the *apostolic testimony* which is found in the New Testament but is not identical with it. This is historical fact. It becomes immediately clear then that a question mark at the end of the title of this book is justified insofar as the historical evidence is taken seriously. Still to be decided is whether this is a matter only of historical study or whether the criterion is also theologically legitimate.

THE ORIGIN OF THE BOOKS
OF THE NEW TESTAMENT

When we inquire about the origin of the individual parts of the New Testament, we come upon questions very similar to those in the beginning of this chapter. There we said that "the New Testament as the church's book" is not only the book which complements the church, but is also the book whose limits have been defined in the church. Now it must be added that the New Testament is also the book that originated in and through the church since its individual parts were the work of churchmen. If that is true, the problems are intensified. Before taking this up I want to direct attention to a few items familiar to theologians which the reader should also know about if certain conclusions are to be based upon them in a later part of this study. Let me emphasize that I am not going to introduce special hypotheses here. I merely want to speak about some of the results which New Testament scholarship considers indisputable (many of which, in fact, have been considered so for a long time). Our main concern is with the overall picture, so that a small difference of opinion here or there will not matter.

The New Testament as a Collection of Writings

We may begin with the simple statement that the New Testament is not a unity, referring for the moment only to its literary character and not to its contents. In its present form the New Testament consists of twenty-seven individual writings, which in itself is not without some significance as one example will show. At the end of the Revelation of John, the last book in the New Testament today, these words are found: "I warn every one who hears the words of the prophecy of this book: if any one adds to them, God will add to him the plagues described in this book, and if any one takes away from the words of the book of this prophecy, God will take away his share in the tree of life and in the holy city, which are described in this book" (Rev. 22:18–19). The fact that these are the third and fourth final verses in the New Testament has sometimes led to the identification of "this book" with the New Testament or even the entire Bible. And this has inspired emotional sermons which warn that whoever takes anything away from the New Testament or the Bible sins against God. These verses have also been taken as the basis for the indestructibility of the entire Bible. But this is faulty reasoning, for the phrase "words of the prophecy of this book" clearly refers exclusively to the Revelation of John as a unit by itself and to nothing else.

There is a second point to consider here. The order of the New Testament writings, as it developed in the course of the history of the canon and as it appears today, seems at first glance to be due to chronology. The New Testament opens with the Gospels which describe the work of Jesus. There follow in succession the story of the church's origins in Acts, twenty-one writings which are letters (or make use of the epistolary form) through which the apostles address the church, and finally, the outline of future events in Revelation. This has all the appearance of a planned arrangement—in fact I do not see how this can be denied. But we must distinguish between the contents of a writing and the time of its composition. The sequence in the New Testament is simply an ordering according to literary genre and provides no hints about dates.

This is another reason why the interpretation of Revelation 22:18–19 just mentioned is grossly inadequate. Second Peter, part of the present canon, most certainly was written after Revelation. Its author, therefore, would have added something to whatever canon the author of Revelation could have had in mind and would have brought down upon himself the plagues described in Revelation—if, of course, the writer of Revelation had really intended to conclude the New Testament (as he knew it) with the thought some have occasionally attached to his words.

The New Testament should not be understood in this light because it is a collection of different writings composed at different times with no common author. It does not form a literary unity which gives the reader the right to jump from one writing to another as though it were. And it is most important to remember that the writings in the canon have not been placed there in chronological order, so that we have to distinguish between content and time of composition. It will be helpful now to arrange the twenty-seven books according to the order in which they were written, being careful not to be influenced by the contents. Since none of the writings can be dated by direct means, we are dependent upon indirect criteria in assigning dates.

It should be no surprise that historians are not in complete agreement here, yet one result does stand firm: the letters of Paul are older than the Gospels in their present form. Even though Paul was closer to Jesus in time than were the Gospel writers, we learn practically nothing about Jesus from him! This rather amazing fact will have some bearing on later discussions, for it means that the picture of Jesus in the Gospels was not drawn until a time considerably later than the events themselves.

Most scholars agree that the oldest writing in the New Testament is Paul's Letter to the church of Thessalonica (1 Thessalonians), very probably written at Corinth around A.D. 50. His remaining letters follow this approximate order: the Letter to the Galatians, the Letter to the Philippians (in its present form it is most likely a conflation of several letters sent to Philippi), the Letter to Philemon, the Letters to the Corinthians (in all probability 2 Corinthians is a combination of five letters of Paul to Corinth and not an original unity), and the Letter to the Romans. These are the oldest New Testament writings and were written within a period of five or six years in Ephesus, Macedonia, and Achaia near the end of the apostle's active life.

The other letters in the New Testament bearing Paul's name were almost certainly written by his disciples. This may strike us as strange or even as a downright falsification, but in antiquity the attitudes towards authorship were different from ours. Often a student would produce a work in the name of his teacher from whom the core of the material was taken—in fact, this could even be a sign of modesty. It would be anachronistic for us to judge such pseudonymity by our ethical standards. Furthermore, we should keep in mind a point we have already touched upon, namely, the church desired to stand within the stream of apostolic tradition. We can imagine the reasoning of the early Christians: the apostle Paul is dead and now his followers write what they think he would have said if he were in their situation.

As their model, the authors of the Gospels of Matthew and Luke used the Gospel of Mark which followed Paul's letters and was probably written just before A.D. 70. Matthew, Luke, and Mark, the oldest Gospel, are called the synoptic Gospels. The Gospel of Matthew may have been written in the eighties while the Gospel of Luke was somewhat later but certainly before the turn of the century. Later, the author of Luke's Gospel also wrote the Acts of the Apostles. The Gospel of John with its distinctive characteristics when compared with the other three Gospels was quite certainly written before A.D. 100.

The Pauline Letters not by Paul himself are called Deutero-Pauline, the oldest of which is probably 2 Thessalonians dating somewhere in the sixties. The Letters to the Colossians and the Ephesians also belong to the first century while the so-called pastoral Letters (1 and 2 Timothy and Titus) most likely were written at the beginning of the second century. The so-called catholic Epistles are addressed to the church at large and not to one church or a group of churches as are the Pauline Letters. First Peter may confidently be placed in the first century and probably also the Letter of James. The three Letters of John were composed in the second century as well as the Letter of Jude and 2 Peter (the latest writing in the New Testament canon) which should be assigned a time around A.D. 130–140. The Revelation of John, in a class by itself, was written during the period A.D. 90–100. The Letter to the Hebrews may also have been written around the same time, or perhaps, even somewhat earlier.

Some Implications

At the beginning of this section I said that the New Testament came into existence in and through the church with its individual parts being composed between A.D. 50 and A.D. 130–140. No one would suggest that there was no Christian church before A.D. 150. But if we admit this, it takes the edge off our pride in the Protestant principle of *sola scriptura* which we usually hold up against the Roman Catholic idea of "Scripture and tradition," because the writings which are considered canonical under the *sola scriptura* rubric arose during the period of early tradition—this is beyond dispute. And we have no answer when we are asked why early tradition is normative but later tradition is not.

There are no grounds at all for an argument that the church suddenly underwent a fundamental change in A.D. 150. If documents that are now authoritative could be produced in the church before 150, why not also after

150? In the previous section the discussion centered only on the collecting and canonization of the writings by the ancient church, but the problem is aggravated as soon as we recognize that none of the writings that were brought together was written at a time when there was no tradition. Ever since the Reformation the idea of "tradition" has been distasteful to Protestants, yet we seem not to have noticed that *sola scriptura* also ties us to tradition we had hoped to avoid, and the Protestant view we have learned and grown up with becomes inadequate and in need of revision. But can it be revised without completely jeopardizing our position?

Tradition in the New Testament

The conclusions we have reached so far have been drawn from very general observations on the writings of the New Testament. Instead of antedating all tradition, the writings originated within the church up to about A.D. 130–140 and, as a closer study shows, were by no means unrelated to one another. The particular occasion of each was the need determined by a particular set of circumstances and a particular group of readers with no mention of any mysterious inspiration guiding the authors who relied instead on already existing material, incorporating it into their writings in a variety of ways. We should have some awareness of how they went about this.

Many of the writings in the New Testament display an unmistakable literary dependence upon earlier material. A good example of this is the second chapter of 2 Peter which is almost identical with the Letter of Jude. The author of 2 Peter was obviously familiar with the Letter of Jude and used it in his own letter. (A number of reasons suggests that the relationship is not to be explained by the other possibility, viz., Jude made use of 2 Peter.) I have already said that Matthew and Luke must have known the Gospel of Mark, since Mark's narratives occur in both Matthew and Luke in nearly complete form and, to a great degree, in the same order in which they are found in Mark. In addition to their use of Marcan material both of these Gospels contain (almost) identical sayings of Jesus, a phenomenon to be explained only by assuming that they had at their disposal a common model or pattern. Scholars have called this a "sayings source," since it appears to have consisted mainly of sayings of Jesus.

The dependence of 2 Peter on Jude and of Matthew and Luke on Mark can be demonstrated, since both Jude and Mark have come down to us as independent sources. Matthew's and Luke's use of a sayings source (abbreviated as Q) is only a conjecture, although one of high probability. The prototype pattern of sayings is easily reconstructed from the non-narrative material of Mark that is common to both Gospels. This dependence of Matthew and Luke upon two sources has led scholars to speak of the "two-sources hypothesis," and may be illustrated as follows:

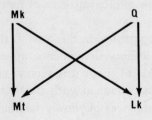

The relationship of Matthew and Luke to a sayings source is not without parallels in the New Testament. The reliance of other writings upon models can be shown with a high degree of certainty, even though such models no longer exist as independent units. First Peter, for example, may have utilized already existing material containing admonitions to baptismal candidates (1 Peter 1:3–4:11) and set it within an epistolary frame (1:1 f. and 4:12 ff.). There can be little doubt that the author of Acts also drew from sources, and even very early writings show evidence of such dependence. Paul, for instance, often makes explicit reference to older units of tradition (1 Cor. 11:23 ff. and 1 Cor. 15:3 ff.). We may also observe that during this early period the Gospel of Mark (the model for Matthew and Luke) did not come from one hand but was itself indebted to several sources. Additional examples can be marshalled which make clear the relationship of parts of the New Testament to older tradition; later sections seek their roots in the past by incorporating, quoting, or appealing to tradition.

This looking back to the past was accomplished not only by using already formulated material but also by a quite different technique, which nevertheless still pointed in the same direction. Earlier I stated that letters were published in Paul's name by individuals who reasoned that if Paul had still been living, he would have decided thus and so and would have written the kind of letter they wrote. In these Deutero-Pauline Letters it is not difficult to recognize the presence and development of Pauline thoughts, so that in a twofold way there is a tie with the past, as Pauline thoughts are worked in and the letter written in Paul's name. The same steps appear with the so-called catholic Letters. They carry in their titles the names of James, Jude, and Peter, yet none was written by them. Why then are these names ascribed to the letters? There are differences of detail for each letter, of course, but the titles gave common expression to the desire of the later church to have the apostles of old speak. It was the church's conviction that it was bound to the older tradition, indeed, to the *apostolic* tradition. This principle—whatever is apostolic is normative or canonical—we have already met in the discussion on the limits of the canon.

The feelings about "apostolicity" (in the sense we have just been using it) come to the surface for the first time in the marginal areas of the New Testament. Not until a relatively late date (in the Deutero-Pauline and catholic Letters) was the claim of apostolic authorship put forth to establish the legitimacy of (later) writings; the purpose was not to deceive, but to stamp these later writings as apostolic. Pseudonymity assigned a value to the contents of the writings and was never intended to be taken as a historical statement on the actual authorship. This attitude which became explicit in the later New Testament age can also be found (although only implicitly) in the earlier writings of the New Testament wherever older traditions were used to satisfy the obligation felt by Christians of looking back to the past. But in both early and late writings the same interest in preserving or emphasizing the link with the past is present even though different means of expressing it were used. This is what I meant when I said that Christians felt bound to apostolic tradition.

Variation in the New Testament

The question may now be raised: Why were older formulas not repeated simply by quoting them? Why were they altered instead? In Matthew and Luke the Gospel of Mark is not merely copied, but is rewritten and in the process changed (in places, profoundly so). The Deutero-Pauline Letters incorporate Pauline ideas in such a way that they either are expanded or invested with new interpretations. And when the author of 2 Peter made use of the Letter of Jude, he did not leave it in its original form but introduced several changes. Similar examples can be found in nearly all of the New Testament books. In short, as ancient (i.e., apostolic) tradition was passed along, it was modified, and we may very well wonder why.

The answer is very simple. Tradition was altered because it apparently was not satisfactory to quote older expressions as they stood. This was clearly the case as "Christianity" was required to adopt the Greek language and drop Aramaic (a late form of Hebrew spoken in Palestine in Jesus' day). Soon after the circle of Hellenistic Jewish-Christians was forced out of Jerusalem following Stephen's death (Acts 11:19 ff.), the mission to the Gentiles was begun in Antioch; Paul later took up the work on a large scale, and this brought the problem of language to center stage.

Anyone who has ever translated a text knows that it should not be done word for word. With modern languages that are closely related this is impossible, to say nothing of attempting it with completely different languages, as in the translation from a Semitic (Aramaic) to an Indo-

Germanic (Greek) tongue. The translator is troubled
here not only with another language, but another culture
and another way of thinking as well. If he wants to be
understood, he will not be able to avoid, in the long run,
completely restating the older expressions in contemporary form.

In many places in the New Testament an Aramaic
original is discernible in the Greek text, especially where
the translation into Greek is quite literal. Literal translation was not the rule, however, and in most cases another
(and admittedly better) method was followed. There
was not only translation but a "bringing over" of concepts, as translators availed themselves of the new world
of ideas. In Palestine Jesus was called rabbi, Messiah,
and Son of God, but these terms could not always be
used in addressing the Greek mind, because to many
they were unknown. Messiah was literally translated as
"Christ," but very quickly ceased to be an honorific title
and practically became a name. "Son of God" was also
literally translated, but in the Greek-Hellenistic world
Son of God had a very different meaning than it did in
Palestinian-Jewish thought (this will be discussed more
fully later). On the other hand, completely new ideas
were introduced, such as *soter* (Saviour), for example,
which did not exist in the Palestinian milieu, or *kyrios*
(Lord), which referred to cultic deities in the Greek-
Hellenistic world.

Several other examples give evidence of the same practice. When the matter of divorce arose in Palestine, it
was always within the context of Jewish marriage laws.
According to Jewish law only the husband was permitted
to divorce himself from his wife; this he did by present-

ing her with a letter of divorce. But Hellenistic and
Roman laws also gave the wife the right to divorce her
husband. What would be more understandable, then,
than to change an original statement on divorce and
speak of it in this new light? This is the case in Mark
10:1–12. The passage divides into two sections. The first,
verses 1–9, represents the purely Jewish view: May a
man divorce his wife with a letter of divorce? The question is posed and then answered: "What therefore God
has joined together, let not man put asunder." But a
second section, verses 10–12, follows, even though the
question has been satisfactorily answered: "In the house
the disciples asked him again about this matter." One
wonders why they brought it up again since there could
hardly have been any misunderstanding! Jesus' answer,
however, shows why the problem has to be mentioned
again: "And he said to them, 'Whoever divorces his wife
and marries another, commits adultery against her; and
if *she* divorces her husband and marries another, *she*
commits adultery'." The question is reintroduced because
Hellenistic and Roman law must be taken into considera-
tion. No new or different grounds are sanctioned and the
traditional attitude is simply restated, but now with Hellenistic and Roman law in mind. It is quite clear that
Jesus did not speak these words since his concern was
only with Palestinian-Jewish law. We can only conclude
that an older tradition was later altered, and in the case
here, by adding to it.

It should be readily conceded that the altering of older
tradition was the only appropriate way of expressing it
correctly in another language. Only by reformulating
and not translating literally could the original intent be

preserved in the foreign tongue of another culture with
its own world of ideas, legal system, and so forth. A
literal translation, instead of faithfully passing along an
idea of one language, often placed it in danger of being
lost or, at least, of being obscured.

The church, however, had to reckon not only with the
problem of language, but with the passing of time as
well, and this faced it with new difficulties. It is certain
that in the earliest period of its history the church believed that Jesus would return very soon. This imminent
expectation of the ancient church is called the parousia.
The clearest evidence for it comes from Paul who writes
in 1 Corinthians 15:51: "Lo! I tell you a mystery. We
shall not all sleep, but we shall all be changed." Along
with the parousia of Jesus the end of the world was
expected, and Paul was convinced that during his lifetime the kingdom of God would break in. But an expectation of such events could not be sustained, for, at least
by the second generation of Christians and at the latest
by the third, it was all too obvious that time was march-
ing on. Not only were Christians experiencing time, they
were also becoming quite aware of its passage. As they
reflected on this, it became necessary to think about
matters which had earlier been of no concern to them.
Suddenly there was a need to draw up something like
church ordinances, for example, as the pastoral Letters
(1 and 2 Timothy and Titus) bear witness. Even though
I (with the majority of German New Testament scholars) am of the opinion that the pastorals are Deutero-
Pauline, that is, not from Paul, I believe that their basic
material would not have been different if Paul himself
had written them. The problems appearing in the pas-

toral Letters were of late origin and show that the church had to prepare for a long stay on earth, something it had not previously anticipated.

Because the earliest Christians looked for the parousia in their lifetime, they were not troubled with the problem which is understandably quite real to us: What about death and what follows? Their attitude toward these questions is shown quite plainly in 1 Thessalonians 4:13–18. Several individuals in the Thessalonian church had died, and the church asks Paul what is in store for them. From the viewpoint of the very early church this worry is certainly justifiable, since those who had died could no longer hope to take part in the parousia. Paul himself had been in Thessalonica and had even founded the church there, yet its members had no idea of what would happen to their dead! Apparently he had not touched on this matter while he was among them.

We do not know whether it was in A.D. 50 that Paul first had to deal with the issue of Christians who died before the parousia or whether he was confronted with the problem earlier. He wrote no earlier letters that could give us information here, but this much is certainly true: the problem was not at the center of his preaching, otherwise the statements in 1 Thessalonians would not make sense. In any case it is the passing of time that makes the problem acute as the return of Jesus was delayed longer than had originally been expected.

It is worth noting, however, that despite the situation at Thessalonica the problem of the resurrection of the dead remained a marginal concern in Paul's theology. In 1 Thessalonians 4:13 ff. he says that those who are alive and remain at the time of the parousia will be caught up in the air together with the dead who will have risen first. He is referring to all Christians who are alive at the time he writes, so that to die before the parousia is really an exception. On the other hand, in 1 Corinthians, written several years later, he fully reckons with the fact that of those who are still alive several (but not all!) will die before the parousia: "We shall not all sleep, but we shall all be changed" (1 Cor. 15:51). What is new here, as the context of 1 Corinthians 15 makes clear, is the thought that the living, too, will be changed. Nevertheless, this teaching stands definitely on the periphery and is by no means as central as we with our concern with death would have expected it to be.

THE NEW TESTAMENT AS THE CHURCH'S EARLIEST EXTANT VOLUME OF PREACHING

The very early church, aware of the passage of time, was compelled to develop and reshape its message, since it could not simply pass it along literally in its original form. Issues which had not (yet) appeared earlier became important and demanded attention (whether the church faced this task willingly or not is not important). Time and circumstances changed, so that the older form of the message had to be modified. Even the second generation of Christians—and certainly the third and subsequent generations—had to be addressed differently than was the first. This would be obviously even more urgent if later generations were part of another cultural milieu and were accustomed to different ideas and concepts. Each writing of the New Testament has its own place in the history of the early church's preaching. The development or reformulation of tradition was always an accommodation to new circumstances and new conditions. This is as true for the development of the teaching of Jesus (on divorce, for example) as for the progression of thought in Pauline theology as seen in his successive letters. And it is as true for the jump from Paul to the Deutero-Pauline Letters (recall what I said about the need for office and ordinances in the pastoral Letters) as it is for the relationship of the Gospel of Mark to the Gospels of Matthew and Luke.

Let me say something further on the Gospels. As the church unexpectedly continues on earth, Luke is forced to deal with the problem of a delayed parousia. In the beginning it was not "forseen" that the church would ever have a history, so Luke now has to find the proper place for this history of the church in the course of the overall history of the world. He reflects upon the past and develops a scheme of sacred history in which the life of Jesus belongs to the past while the church (in Acts) is on the way to the parousia which, however, will not occur until sometime in the distant future. Matthew, in a completely different situation, has to tailor the message for a Jewish-Christian audience; hence, more intensely than anyone before him, he works with the Old Testament. Common to both Matthew and Luke is their restating of Mark's Gospel in such a way that each is able to address himself to the particular problems of his own readers.

The same tendency is found in the catholic Letters. We can take 2 Peter, the latest of these letters, as one example. Among other things, the author wrestles with the continuing problem of a parousia which has still not taken place and which supplies fuel to the mockers. It is explicitly argued here that there are times when older traditions not only may not be helpful, but may be downright troublesome. His opponents appeal to Paul but, says the author, they twist his words. The rebuke brings to mind the problem of preambles to church ordinances I mentioned in the Introduction. I suggested there that referring to a text is utterly meaningless if no directions are given on how to interpret it correctly. Both the author of 2 Peter and his opponents turn to the same texts—the letters of Paul—but each understands them in a different light. One simply cannot repeat Paul literally. But how then does one use his statements properly and make them relevant for a later period?

The author of 2 Peter claims that his tradition alone correctly understands Paul. In actual fact, however, it is his opponents who are historically more correct but they draw from their understanding the wrong implications for personal conduct in this later period for the church's history. A later generation cannot directly utilize older writings without first bridging the temporal gap, and this is done either through an interpretation of that literature or by altering the older tradition. In this sense the writings of the New Testament represent a variation and a reformulation of older tradition to meet the need of specific circumstances. Hence we say that the New Testament is the oldest extant volume of the preaching of the church.

General Principles and Specific Statements

There is something liberating about this distinction. Paradoxically, the problems it raises make our relationship to the New Testament more difficult and, to some degree, easier. The unprejudiced and even slightly observant reader knows that there are many contradictions in the New Testament. I do not want to list them here except to mention the best-known example. Romans 3:28 says: "For we hold that a man is justified by faith apart from works of law," or as Luther has correctly and pertinently translated: "For we hold that a man is justified apart from the works of the law—by faith alone." God justifies the man who believes. He then seeks his security in this gift which undergirds and sustains his spiritual life. But opposed to this is James 2:24 which seems to be a clear contradiction: "You see that a man is justified by works and *not by faith alone.*" In fact, it even looks as though James 2:24 were directed against Paul.

The contradiction disappears when we consider to whom each statement is made. Paul is addressing the man who thinks he has to do something to acquire justification and is convinced that he bears complete responsibility for obtaining it. The apostle's response to this is a resounding No! It is God who justifies. Whoever thinks he is able to do anything to acquire a gift shows disrespect for the giver, and for Paul in the case here this is blasphemy against God. There is a danger, however, if these thoughts of Paul become a watchword and are assumed to be a general truth or a *general principle.* If we forget they form a *specific statement* to a particular audience, they could be used to support the notion that personal effort is useless, even in the best of lives; and if this pious attitude should lead to complete inactivity, the result would be ethical libertinism. But the individual who is indifferent to personal effort completely reverses the thought of Paul, who never disregarded ethics. If the most a person ever says is: "I truly believe that God provides justification," he is not talking of faith as Paul did for whom faith included the entire life. Libertines can find no comfort in either writer, for the statement in James also relates faith to life and in a sense is almost Pauline even though it has a completely different ring. What appears at first glance to be a contradiction vanishes if both principles are understood as *specific statements* to a particular group of people at a particular place in the history of the preaching of the early church.

As a rule of thumb I should like to suggest the following: If you come across contradictory *principles* in the New Testament, first of all try to determine when and to whom the *specific statements* were made. Not until you understand what the situation was in which a principle was declared can you know how it is to be understood. In practically every case you will discover that apparent contradictions disappear if each principle is read as a specific statement related to particular conditions. It would in fact be quite remarkable if there were no "contradictions" in the New Testament. An illustration will make this clear. The different books of the New Testament were written over a span of eighty years. It makes little difference to us today whether a text is 1,840 or 1,920 years old, but translated into present-day terms, these eighty years would represent the period from 1890 up to now, and it would mean that 1 Thessalonians was written in 1890 and 2 Peter in 1970. Suppose now a modern book is published containing twenty-seven sermons encompassing this period of time. We would immediately be aware that pre-World War I sermons would in general no longer have any meaning for us. If you were to read an older book of sermons, you would see this at once.

The more pointed, the timelier, and consequently, the better the sermons were for that day, the less relevant they would be for us today. In fact, many would give us good cause to wonder at their neglect of issues that now trouble us, as, for example, the relationship of church and state, social questions, attitude toward war, etc. We would have to be careful not to judge them with our presuppositions, since the standard of measurement could never be whether they are relevant to *us* or speak to *us* but whether they were relevant *in their day*. Such sermons could not—and were not intended to—speak to us. Therefore, in such a book of sermons divergent and even directly conflicting principles would ·not necessarily mean they were really contradictory.

Summary: If we take seriously the fact that the preaching recorded in the New Testament occurred in very specific historical situations, we will be kept from too quickly labelling opposing principles as contradictions. By accepting this, historical study actually eases some of the problems.

The Problem of the Interval of Time and Space

A number of problems still exist which make our study of the New Testament difficult. We can, for example, no longer make the uncritical statement that the New Testament is "God's Word," implying that God has spoken here and, therefore, because it is God's Word, it concerns us and we must heed it and think of it as addressed to us.

In the controversy with those factions in the church mentioned at the beginning of the book, the following question is always framed as an alternative: *Is* the Bible God's Word or does it *contain* God's Word? If the discussion is restricted to the New Testament, the alternative becomes: Is the New Testament God's Word or does it contain God's Word? The purpose of the question is obvious. If we must accept the New Testament as it stands as the Word of God to its readers (of today), then it *is* God's Word. But if it is necessary to eliminate certain points so that the reader does not encounter God's Word until the critic's sifting process is completed, then the New Testament only *contains* God's Word. The alternative, however, is not correctly formulated, and for this reason I refuse to answer the question (while it is in the form of an alternative). A faulty procedure like this obscures the real nature of the problem. One should first determine whether a question is really possible as a question, especially if alternatives are included. If this is overlooked and answers given too quickly, one may assent to the (possibly false) presuppositions of the questioner. Some questions cannot be answered until they are constructed correctly or at least put in proper perspective.

Is the New Testament the Word of God or does it contain the Word of God? This can be answered only when it is clear what is understood by the expression "Word of God" since what it means to me can be quite different from what it means to someone else (as the example of Romans 3:28 and James 2:24 shows). For this reason I prefer to consider the question in sections. Is the New Testament the Word of God? If this is asking whether it is the Word of God for *me*, I must answer No, because no part of it was written expressly for me. Does the New Testament contain the Word of God? Yes, because from it I am addressed. Both questions can be brought together by keeping this important point in mind: The New Testament contains God's Word for me as I meet it in the form of messages to others. It is not simply the Word of God as a direct communication to me; quite the contrary, every book of the New Testament claims to be the Word of God for specific readers of that day. It is, therefore, the Word of God, but not for me. It *becomes* the Word of God *for me* when I restate those ancient messages in modern terms by acceptable methods (still to be discussed).

This superficially conceived alternative overlooks the historical character of the New Testament. I never possess the Word of God in a timeless sense, because at every point it is related to historical situations, and when I seek it in the New Testament, I always find it separated from me in distance and time. Only by trying to understand the individual writings as messages to audiences of the past of whom I have never been a part do I read the New Testament properly. The task of exegesis is to explain those ancient messages which were addressed to readers of their day, but the result will never be a message for me. The eventual goal should be to provide me with a message, but before that is achieved a number of additional steps requiring careful use must be considered. For now it is enough to warn against hasty conclusions.

Suppose for a moment that Paul wrote his passionate Letter to the Galatians and his sober First Letter to the Thessalonians at the same time but somehow mixed up the addresses. Both churches would have read the letters (both apostolic) at their worship services—quite possibly in one continuous reading—but neither would have felt that Paul had been speaking directly to it. Having concluded from the letter how matters stood in the other church, each church, to be sure, would have understood what Paul had in mind, but that is all! Each congregation would have knowledge of a situation far removed from it, but neither could accept Paul's words as a personal message. In order for the message to come alive, each church would need to think about how the ideas intended for the other were to be applied to its own situation.

If what I have just said is true for the two letters as complete units, we must then be just as careful when we study only one small part of a letter. For not until we have some idea of the overall contents can we understand the individual paragraph. When we receive a letter of several pages today, we do not read the first page only on the first day, the second page the next day and so on; we read it in its entirety and then try to understand the parts in terms of the whole. I have the impression that current practice in the church is often quite different. The reader selects a small portion of the New Testament here, another there, often nothing more than a single verse, as a proof text, for example, or for his own meditation. He feels this is justifiable because he ascribes to the New Testament the (not historically understood) concept of the "Word of God," and is convinced that each verse is intended directly for him. This completely overlooks two facts, however: (1) The fraction of the letter under study can be properly understood only in its relationship to the whole (the letter itself, not the entire New Testament!), and, (2) the letter was originally addressed to others. I consider it unacceptable, therefore, to quote isolated sentences from the Scriptures as a basis for the formulation of dogma. Nearly always the individual expression is applied improperly with no attention given to the original historical situation or the context.

Summary: The individual writings of the New Testament are of value to us only if they are first read as documents geographically and temporally separated from us. They must be left in their own age and understood as products of their time, and not until I see this will I be able to determine what yesterday's message can say to me today. The problem is not solved by the simple assumption that the New Testament is addressed to me personally; as a matter of fact, this makes the reading of the Bible more difficult. I have only these two choices: either I read the Bible properly, even though this is more difficult, or improperly because it is easier. I for my part cannot recommend an improper course simply because it is easier.

The Limits of the Canon

The subject of the limits of the canon was introduced again when I said that the New Testament is the oldest extant volume containing the preaching of the church.

The New Testament consists of documents that are records of the history of the earliest Christian preaching, but that history, instead of ending with the New Testament, continued on. Furthermore, there are other written records of the early church's preaching that antedate much of the preaching now found in the New Testament. One indisputable example is the First Epistle of Clement to the Corinthians which was not written by an apostle and does not pretend to be, but whose lack of apostolic authorship is not a convincing objection to it since, as we have clearly seen, there are doubts about the apostolic authorship of a good many letters that have made their way into the New Testament.

We face a complete impasse in trying to justify the limits of the canon if we describe the New Testament as the oldest extant volume of the church's preaching. Someone could easily insist that there is also a second, a third, and a fourth volume, and that even the choice of material to be included in the first volume hinges more on practical concerns than on objective judgment. And this, one could argue, would raise the specter of a hopeless relativism.

Summary: Earlier I said that the limits of the canon are fluid; I meant by this that there should be such limits and that they are approximately the same as the ones we recognize today. But if the New Testament is considered to be the oldest record of preaching, then those limits are completely irrelevant, for the latest modern book of sermons could, if we were able to overcome all the technical problems, also be bound up with that first volume, and we would no longer be able to think of objectively determined limits.

The Norm

The last section introduces an entirely new topic. Suppose that all the sermons ever preached or printed under Christian auspices were collected in a single volume. Among them there would be some sermons we would look upon as strange because they were historically removed from us; but there would also be others (also strange to us) that would be theologically unacceptable in our eyes, or heretical or false (or whatever designation we want). Consider the differences that have often existed in the church. I am not saying here that the Protestant Christian labels every Catholic sermon false or that the Catholic Christian labels every Protestant sermon false. But we cannot deny that each side is responsible for sermons the other must hold as false according to its own presuppositions. The conclusion follows that a sermon must be measured against some norm if it is to be considered theologically correct. Merely preaching it is no assurance that it is correct.

In view of our discussion up to this point, it would be misleading to argue that the New Testament should be that decisive norm for preaching, since it is itself a volume of preaching. It is also not clear why the preaching from the period between A.D. 50 and A.D. 130 can stand as correct with no questions asked but what is later than A.D. 130 (or even earlier, as 1 Clement, for example) must be examined for its soundness. Why such a sharp line of demarcation in A.D. 130? From our deliberations it would seem that even the preaching of the earlier period, including what is in the New Testament, ought to be examined to see if it was appropriate and relevant, although not to see if it is relevant for us. The concern

of whether such preaching is "for us" should never come
into question. It is more important to ask whether the
ancient preaching found in the New Testament made its
point for the listeners of that day. We cannot rule out
the possibility that there may be false teaching in it, so
that our task is to find some criterion for judgment.

We have emphasized that the variety in the New
Testament is due to the different times and different cul-
tures to which the writings belonged. But does it follow
from this that each new age determines what can be
said? The question uncovers a real danger. I only need
to recall how Paul's well-known words—"To the Jews I
became as a Jew and to the Greeks as a Greek"—and
Luther's attitude that he was on the scene on behalf of
his precious Germans were interpreted during the Third
Reich to mean that a "German Gospel" should be proclaimed. The thought was not that the Gospel should be
expressed in a German milieu for Germans in German
(there would be no quarrel with that), but that it should
be made to comport with the German character (as it
was understood then). The Gospel was supposed to fit in
with Nordic, Aryan people, with the result that Jews,
naturally, could no longer belong to the church. Here,
the (admittedly new) situation in which the Gospel was
to be preached took precedence over the Gospel itself. In
a later age or in a different environment the Gospel does
indeed make use of a language that will be understood
in the new milieu, *but this language cannot be allowed to
define what the Gospel is.*

A few examples from the period between the age of
the New Testament and now will add some light to the

problem which is by no means a modern one. During the Middle Ages Aristotelian thought was prominent and Aristotelian categories could be used in defining the real presence in the Lord's Supper. Out of this the teaching of transubstantiation arose. At the time it was perfectly acceptable to preach and teach this, but today the Aristotelian base has fallen away and other categories must be found for expressing the real presence. If Aristotelianism is still taken today as the only adequate vehicle for discussing the idea, it means that the attitudes of around A.D. 1215 prevail over the original subject matter. In other words, a thirteenth century concept about which nothing was known in Palestine in Jesus' day, which played no role in the Graeco-Roman world of the first century, and which is outmoded even today takes precedence over the original concept. The interpretation that could have been appropriate in 1215 and in fact was not only permissible but most likely also correct and necessary for that day has actually replaced the original subject matter.

A full discussion of the real presence in the Lord's Supper would take us from the main theme, since background material and completely different problems are involved. I am more concerned that we recognize the following principle: An interpretation must avail itself of concepts and ideas that can be understood. But concepts and ideas change (as our world view, for example), so that one must be on guard lest the interpretation subtly push aside the original subject itself.

It is quite possible of course to interpret an earlier interpretation, but the greatest caution must be exercised here. An earlier interpretation cannot simply be used as the base for a later one, since the original subject matter would then be seen only through the glasses of the earlier interpretation. It is wiser to begin afresh with the subject itself, making use, naturally, of earlier interpretations in order to be apprised of other attempts to understand the original subject matter. This will preclude the danger of being too strongly influenced by an interpretation that was conditioned by its times and of giving it such prestige that it dims the original theme. If I do rigidly settle upon a particular interpretation (whether willingly or not is immaterial), I would obscure the subject which lies behind the interpretation and which will always be larger, more varied, and more complex than any one of its interpretations.

The formulating of dogma in a final form would seem to be, then, a hopeless task, since it ties future generations to the categories of the past. Anyone today who insists upon stating dogma this way overrates his abilities as an interpreter, although we can understand why this was the usual procedure in earlier periods. Critical methods were not yet known and the use of absolute terms was nothing more than a sign of the intensity with which ideas were held to be true and correct. But the intellectually honest man of the twentieth century who still clings to those older ideas will be encumbered by so much past interpretation that he would really be better off to put down his ideas in his own words at the start. This is by no means a problem for the Roman Catholics alone! We would do well to ponder how our own creeds of an earlier day are to be used properly.

We may think that the Augsburg Confession of 1530 was, at the time, an appropriate statement of Christian truth and we may feel free to interpret it today. But we have no right to insist that our interpretation will be the only satisfactory declaration of Christian truth for the future. Even if the Apostles' Creed, for example, is taken as the basis of a modern interpretation, it is still an inadmissible conclusion that that interpretation must necessarily be a proper contemporary expression of the Christian faith. The purpose of all creedal formulas has been to express Christian faith and truth for their own age. The men who drafted them quite naturally had to use the language and thoughts of their day if they hoped to provide answers to questions that were important then. The difficulties this presents would not be eased by seeking security in established church decisions and creeds, since the church, too, has always been limited in the art of interpretation by the language available at the time. Furthermore, it has never been possible to decide in advance what forms of expression will be suitable for a future age. This is as true for the church of the Reformation as it is for the Roman church and for the ancient church which was responsible for the Apostles' Creed.

If the variation in the preaching recorded in the New Testament was due to ever-changing environments which called for new modes of expression, the new environments nevertheless were never allowed to become so influential that the original subject matter was overshadowed. In line with this we can make the following preliminary suggestion: that preaching is theologically acceptable which expresses the original subject matter in each new situation in such a way that it is capable of being understood by its new audience.

This raises the very basic question of what the "subject matter" is. But before we try to answer it, one could ask whether it is even possible to make any kind of formulation here. Will the subject matter not be completely lost to us (or, at least will not such a danger exist) if we draw up such a forthright formulation?

It will be best to move carefully with the problem, one step at a time. The subject matter is something that has existed beforehand, that lies behind its individual witnesses, and has been passed along from the past. Some of the examples we have already used will be helpful again. In the Deutero-Pauline Letters the subject matter is Pauline ideas which have been taken as a base, reformulated and given out in Paul's name as though they actually came from him. The literary interdependence of many other writings of the New Testament enables us to discover what the subject matter was in older documents which Christians used out of a sense of obligation, and then restated in order to make them "contemporary." In general we can say that the subject matter is the "beginning," although this is admittedly too brief and must be expanded.

We are still concerned only with external forms when we give this beginning an apparent content and say that the subject matter is "Jesus," because "Jesus" is nothing more than a name or a designation. Yet, the clear evidence of the New Testament is that he is indeed the subject matter, and even though the evidence is expressed with luxuriant variety, it is always *he* to whom witness is borne. Throughout the New Testament and in all Christian churches through the ages it is and has been the common conviction that he is the one who is of ultimate importance. In contrast to the sects, the churches have always refused to reduce Jesus to a level where he would become just one among many great individuals. They have also consistently denied recognition to additional revelations which either exclude Jesus or appear after his time. This attitude toward Jesus is shown in several ways; some prefer to say that in Jesus God revealed himself definitively, others, using a Greek term, say that we are dealing with the *ephhapax* ("once and for all") of God's revelation. In any case Christian faith has always confessed that he is the one and only Lord, and because he was so much the center of their thoughts, the early Christians were anxious to express in word what had first been expressed in his person. They achieved this through the proclamation of their messages which have now been gathered together in the New Testament, the church's first book of preaching.

There should be no hesitation now with the following statement: The "canon" of the Christian church is not the New Testament but Jesus. I must quickly add that I have access to Jesus only as the New Testament bears witness to him, and for this reason I do not set him in the place of the New Testament. But the New Testament is not simply identical with Jesus, because what he brought—what we have called the subject matter—has become part of the variety within the New Testament and a part of the history of early Christian preaching.

And this means that it is at least possible (I am not saying it is so) that at times the milieu or local situation blurred the subject matter.

The church's fundamental interest in Jesus meant that its preaching was appropriate only when everything associated with Jesus' mission and message was restated in such a way that his original intention was preserved and made understandable in each new situation. But if preaching must accommodate itself to the cultural area, as it had to, for example, around the turn of the first century, then the preacher may very well insist that in the beginning a Jesus was vitally important, but his message will no longer deal with the original subject matter concerning Jesus. The mere appearance of something in the New Testament is no guarantee that it brings us into touch with the primary elements of Jesus' life and teaching. Yet, it is this that is of such importance. The question of a norm for Christian preaching leads to the alternative "Jesus or the New Testament," but not in the sense that the choices are mutually exclusive. They stand as alternatives insofar as I am compelled to think about one as a guide. Whoever chooses the entire New Testament as his norm has not been radical enough in his inquiry, because he settles for one interpretation (or even several interpretations) of the original event of Jesus and allows that event to be obscured in the same way (as I pointed out) as when dogma, a creedal confession, or the Apostles' Creed is used by Christians today as the norm.

When modern theology is reproved for not believing the Bible, the charge is not unwarranted, although it is questionable whether it really is a reproof. One segment, at least, of modern theology, does not believe in the Bible or the New Testament because it believes in Jesus and finds its orientation in him; this scarcely supports any serious "charge" within the Christian community. The reason why modern theologians study the New Testament critically should always be given in such accusations, instead of poisoning the atmosphere by simply mentioning the results of their critical studies and omitting the rational grounds for such a position.

The ancient church considered as canonical only what was apostolic; the same principle leads to the modern critical approach to the New Testament. For, if Jesus is truly of central importance, only someone who has been in direct contact with him can bear reliable witness. The direct witnesses who did hear and see him were the apostles. But the historical judgments of the church of the third and fourth centuries are then subject to modification today, because of all the writings (in their present form) in the New Testament only the letters of Paul can be called a direct apostolic witness. And even Paul had not known the earthly Jesus, having seen only the Resurrected One.

This compels us to inquire once more about the "apostolic" witness, but now with the insights and methods available to us. In fact, we do this quite in obedience to the principles of the ancient church whose criterion—canonical = apostolic—was a theologically legitimate interest and not some incidental formula.

Summary: "The New Testament as the church's book" is the book containing the initial witness to Jesus in and through the church. The norm for the Christian church and its preaching, however, must always remain Jesus.

2.

The Norm:

Its Apostolic and

Early Christian Witness

In the first chapter I have tried to show how the idea arose in some circles that a question mark should be placed after the statement that the New Testament is the norm or standard of the church. In the second chapter the task will be to determine just how justifiable this question mark is, as over against an uncritical period. After seeing how the old norm has proved to be unsatisfactory, we will take up the question of the new norm.

METHODOLOGY

Since no writing of the New Testament was written before the first Easter, none is a direct witness to Jesus. Each in some degree reflects the influence of Christian experience in the first decades following Easter, and for this reason variation has always been present. If we desire to find out what was revealed in Jesus of Nazareth, we must reckon with a number of difficulties, since this knowledge is possible only when we critically look behind the texts and try to reconstruct the picture of the earthly Jesus in his words and actions.

The Sources

In the study of a historical figure who lived at a particular time and place on this earth, the best course is to use those sources that stood closest in time to the events of his life. In our case such sources would be Paul's letters. It has already been pointed out, however, that Paul reports practically nothing about Jesus and that, furthermore, he is an "apostle" (eye and ear witness) only in a strained sense, since he had seen only the Resurrected One, never Jesus of Nazareth. We should turn to the Gospels then, with the exception of John's Gospel. One of the unanimous results of biblical scholarship is that the Fourth Gospel is so markedly the product of the theological interests of its author that the picture of the earthly Jesus is completely subjected to his theology and thus as a source for the historical Jesus is almost of no value at all.

This leaves only the so-called synoptic Gospels, whose authors are called Mark, Matthew, and Luke. All of the Gospels, including John's, were originally passed along anonymously, the titles now found in the New Testament having been affixed later. Whether or not they are accurate ascriptions does not affect our present study, although the evidence is very strong that they are not. The "two-sources theory" which explains the relationship of the synoptic Gospels to each other would suggest that we should rely only on the Gospel of Mark, the oldest of the Gospels. But this restriction to Mark is not necessary. In Matthew and Luke it is possible to discern a stratum of common material in the Q source that is older than either Matthew or Luke. Furthermore, peculiar to each of these Gospels are elements of tradition which existed before the Gospel was written. Hence, even though the Gospels were composed relatively late, by applying the techniques of literary criticism material can be reconstructed which clearly goes back to an earlier time. In addition, if it is assumed that Mark also used sources—and these are not difficult to recognize in his text—we have other blocks of tradition which quite certainly antedate his Gospel. We gain by this a look into the history of early Christian preaching before the synoptic Gospels were written, and this brings us considerably closer to Jesus.

The reconstruction of earlier preaching cannot be achieved with complete certainty because of the nature of our sources. Mark, Matthew, and Luke were not slavish editors who merely combined the blocks of tradition at hand. They reworked their sources (although far less than John) according to definite patterns by making changes and introducing supplementary material. If we can discover the principles by which the formulation (or reformulation) of the material within a Gospel was determined, we have made a beginning in reversing the process and have moved a step closer to the original form of the tradition. On the other hand, we should recognize that before the individual units of material were incorporated into a Gospel, they had already been shaped according to definite literary laws of forms; by comparing these units we can reconstruct the original elements of tradition which were already undergoing alteration before they were written down.

We find ourselves moving here unavoidably in a circle: the reconstructed individual units enable us to draw conclusions about the changes in the Gospel and, contrariwise, the principles by which similar changes in the Gospels were made allow us to come to some conclusions about the possible earlier form of the individual traditions. It is quite understandable that there would be uncertainties here, but they are not so crippling that the attempt to look behind the Gospels should be given up as hopeless. This is the road that leads us back to the traditions formed before our Gospels were written. And what stands out so clearly when we arrive is that tradition first consisted of small units, each one complete in itself.

The next step is to arrange these reconstructed units in some order so that their history can be followed. To do this, it is necessary to try to recover the oldest material.

The Picture of Jesus in Liberal Theology

The direction of our study makes it reasonable to inquire now about the norm itself. The apostolic witness to the norm can, at best, lead us only to a preliminary level. If we have said that the norm is Jesus, should we not then, after having worked out what the apostolic witness of the norm is, inquire further about how the norm can be expressed? This, however, confronts us with the problem already referred to of whether it is even possible to express or formulate the subject matter.

Liberal theology with roots in the Enlightenment went about its task in the following manner. Its scholars argued that the picture of Jesus in the Gospels is overlaid with dogma due to the influence of the church and is therefore a secondary source having nothing to do with Jesus himself. Liberal theology, committed to Jesus, but not to the description of him drawn by the later

church, insisted that it was necessary to undo the effect
of the church's dogmatic embellishments. If this were
successful, scholars reasoned, they would have a straightforward, simple, and, especially, undogmatic portrait of
Jesus. This was the Jesus they wanted to believe in. In
order to become a Christian, one did not need to accept
the supernatural elements attached to Jesus, or the myths
that were spun about him, or the miraculous events that
were so easily taken as straightforward historical
accounts.

It would be wrong to dismiss this liberal position too
quickly and write if off as rationalistic. A rationalistic
element is quite clearly present insofar as only what fits
into the liberal world view is valid, but this is not the
real error of liberalism. The error is found in another
area, and for the longest time scholars were not able to
recognize it. Even the opponents of liberal theology
overlooked it. In fact, one can show that the opponents
of liberal theology were scarcely less liberal themselves,
at least in their methods. They simply arrived at different
conclusions.

The fault of the liberals in eliminating dogma from the
portrait of Jesus was that they themselves undertook the
work with their own dogmatic premises. They assumed
that the original, true picture of Jesus was devoid of
dogma. But this was not a justifiable assumption. That
dogma attached itself to later tradition is certainly true,
and could quite possibly be peeled away. The real question, however, was what was it like at the beginning?
The presupposition of the liberal inquiry that the earliest
picture of Jesus was free of dogma simply does not

accord with the evidence. Even the oldest tradition about Jesus that we can detect is not without dogmatic elements and was shaped under the influence of a very dogmatic conception which we still must work out.

Form Criticism

The decisive change in the study of the problem was achieved through "form criticism," the examination of the history of the literary forms as they circulated before being written down. Around the close of the nineteenth and the beginning of the twentieth century there were several early advocates of the method, among whom may be mentioned Franz Overbeck, although his work has exercised little influence, and Herman Gunkel who applied the principles to the study of the Old Testament. Form criticism became most prominent when it was taken up immediately after World War I by such New Testament scholars as Karl Ludwig Schmidt, Martin Dibelius, and Rudolf Bultmann. It is based upon the assumption that the Gospel writer presented each event (1) as he was able and (2) as it served his purpose.

As he was able. This does not refer to the author's technical ability to describe events; this is so obvious it needs no discussion. What it does mean is that he was able to record events only within the context of his own cultural milieu.

As it served his purpose. Let me illustrate this with an example. Suppose a man witnesses an automobile accident. In a letter to his wife or children he includes a description of it; he then also provides the police with a written deposition. Now suppose both documents—the letter and the deposition—are laid side by side and only the paragraphs describing the accident are examined. If the salutation of the letter and the official introductory section of the police report are blocked out, it will still be possible to differentiate immediately between the two. Even a cursory reading will reveal the category of each document. In form criticism this is called the *Sitz im Leben*, the situation or setting in life in which a literary document has been written.

The recognition of a setting in life carries with it several ramifications of considerable methodological importance. In the example of the automobile accident, the decisive point is that the complex event which took place before the eyes of the witness has undergone a kind of "sifting process" because of the setting in life. The setting in life does not allow everything to pass through. If the setting in life is the situation or experience of the letter writer, then what would be characteristic of a police file, for example, is of no interest to him at all. Similarly, if the setting in life is the official police report, nothing will be entered that is of the nature of conjecture or impression or that has to do with the mood of the witness; in short, practically everything that gives warmth to a personal letter will be excluded. A third party, then, has knowledge of the event only to the extent that the documents make it available to him. He only gains information about what happened as it is filtered through the particular viewpoint and description in each document. The setting in life, therefore, blocks our direct access to the historical event itself.

When we study a document historically, the first historical datum we come upon is the setting in life. It is, as it were, the only window through which we can look, so that the only view we ever receive of the historical events is the one offered by the setting in life. Therefore, we can never expect documents which have to do with historical events to yield direct information about them. Our first task is to ascertain what the setting in life is; we must try to determine the angle from which the event was described and what fraction of the total was deemed relevant for inclusion by the setting in life. Not until this has been done do we approach the event itself that is described in the document.

When this principle is applied to texts of the New Testament, the setting in life is, in very broad terms, the church after the first Easter. Not a single line of the New Testament (in its present form) was written before Easter. This general statement is not the whole story, as we shall see, if we notice certain distinctive elements in the texts. We can see these by comparing three well-known literary forms.

1. In the story of the tribute money (Mark 12:13–17) the scene is described very briefly. A tricky question is put to Jesus, he has a coin brought to him, he asks whose likeness is on it and then says: "Render to Caesar the things that are Caesar's, and to God the things that are God's." Not one superfluous word clutters the account.

2. Quite different is the story of Jesus walking on the water (Mark 6:45–52) where the description is full and lifelike. The observations of the disciples are mentioned, for example—they thought they saw a ghost, etc.

3. Finally, the accounts of the so-called institution of the Lord's Supper (Mark 14:20–24, Matt. 26, Luke 22, and 1 Cor. 11) simply tell of a meal in which there was the

breaking of the bread at the beginning and the passing
of the cup at the end without a single syllable used to
describe the actual meal (apart from 1 Cor. 11:25). Even
though the central theme is the final meal of Jesus, there
is a complete absence of any description of the moods
or emotions of the event.

How are these striking differences to be explained?
The early church was not interested in "reporting" the
events of Jesus' life. Instead of providing a direct account
of what had happened, its purpose was to show the post-
Easter church how "contemporary" that past was. This
could be accomplished by choosing the form of the
paradigm (a short illustration or model for preaching),
for example, as in the story of the tribute money. Attention was focused on a concise saying which furnished
the text for "preaching" (I am using it in the modern
sense). The presence of such paradigms is evidence that
there were "preachers" in the early church. In the story
of the walking on the water a paradigm was not chosen
as the basis for preaching; instead, the message was
proclaimed by means of vivid narration. From this we
may conclude that there were "narrators" in the early
church. And in the case of the institution of the Lord's
Supper we discover nothing about the meal, but only
about those aspects which assumed cultic importance for
the early church, namely, what happened at the beginning and at the end of the meal. We can conclude, therefore, that a ritual act, the Lord's Supper, was observed
in the early church.

I can refer here only briefly to these matters, but I
think the examples make it clear that the application of

form criticism uncovers sociological data. From the different forms we can theorize about the sociological situations of the early church and, from this, about the following functions that were part of that structure: the church defended itself, as we can see from its use of sayings dealing with controversy; it had ritual, as the accounts of the institution of the Lord's Supper reveal; it had preachers, as shown by the presence of paradigms; and it had narrators or storytellers.

What form criticism opens to us is primarily a relatively lifelike picture of the early church but not of the life of Jesus! Jesus' life is always presented only in accordance with very definite points of view, each of which has been determined by a particular setting in life.

We should be aware of the disappointment caused by the results of form criticism. Form critical study was preceded by the work on the so-called synoptic problem which set forth the two-sources hypothesis. When scholars discovered that Mark was the oldest Gospel, they thought they had finally reached the historical Jesus (according to their liberal presuppositions). Just when they fancied they had arrived at their goal, form criticism appeared. Looking for the historical Jesus, they found instead the setting in life, the early church. Scholars began to see the early church more clearly than ever before, but the more clearly they saw it, the more Jesus was concealed and the more he receded from them. This brought about the realization that (and let this serve as a summary of what has been said so far about form criticism) the early church was interested in the past not as the past, but only to the extent that it could use it to speak to specific, contemporary situations. Günther Bornkamm, the New Testament scholar at Heidelberg, has explained this very incisively: The early church does not want to say who Jesus *was* but who he *is*. Since Easter it has known him as the Resurrected One who is alive, and therefore it has no interest in historical research (For whom would it do this anyway? The parousia was imminent!) but it does engage in preaching. In the language of the theologian it may be expressed as follows: The separate units of tradition which were later incorporated into our synoptic Gospels have a kerygmatic (i.e., having to do with preaching) character. But this means we do not have direct historical accounts.

The Historical Question

We ought not throw out the baby with the bath water at this point. The units of tradition were shaped in the church and for the purpose of preaching but we should not assume that every account must be unhistorical. This would surely be wrong. The primary judgment here is with *literary* questions, with the determination of the "literary genre," and the succinct conclusion we come to is that we are looking at "kerygma" (preaching) and not reporting. But this does not imply that the contents have to be unhistorical.

It would likewise be wrong to suppose from what has been said that we no longer can or *may* examine kerygmatic traditions historically (that is, with regard to the historicity of the contents). Who would keep me from doing this anyway? I certainly have the right to engage in historical inquiry, although if I do, I should admit forthwith that probing like this is foreign to the original intentions of the authors who were interested in preaching and not reporting. This fact quite understandably makes the historical problem extraordinarily difficult, for in my investigations I have to take careful account of methodology since what I want to receive is different from what the authors of the documents wanted to present. And no longer dare I argue that I will consider something historical until the contrary is proved—such an argument is applicable only for documents that pass themselves off as historical. The early Christians were not interested in the past as such and consequently they felt free to make use of stories that were not historical to illustrate the meaning of Jesus for their own day. Therefore, when I take something to be historical I must furnish good reasons for such an opinion and, similarly, I must establish why I hold something to be unhistorical.

We must, however, distinguish between this historical question and the question about truth. For example, in order to illustrate the essence of Bismarck I may use an anecdote that never really occurred in his life. And while it would be quite true that the anecdote was not historical, in a certain sense it would still be "true" in that it threw light on some aspect of his life. This is exactly how the pictures of Jesus in the synoptic tradition are to be understood; their purpose is to highlight the "contemporary" meaning of Jesus for the early church.

In the application of the principles of form criticism, we meet an even greater variety of settings in life than we have considered so far. If it can be shown that a unit of tradition has Palestinian coloring, then it most likely has to do with a special problem affecting the early church in Palestine. The particular traditions of the Palestinian church, such as sayings dealing with controversy, can be distinguished from those of the Hellenistic church, such as nature miracles, for example. And secondary additions (e.g., as in the paragraph on divorce) in a unit of tradition point to a still different setting in life. Thus the individual units of tradition which circulated prior to our synoptic Gospels not only existed independently with regard to time, place, and contents, but can be placed in categories. Form critical study affords a view into the history of the preaching of the early church, a history that had already begun before our New Testament, which can be traced through the New Testament, and which continued after the New Testament.

If we are successful in classifying this pre-synoptic material, we can make our way through the New Testament, especially through the synoptic Gospels and the traditions they utilized, and penetrate to the earliest layer of tradition which will turn out to be kerygma, preaching. This may bring us much closer to Jesus than before, but we still have not yet reached back directly to Jesus himself!

This should be evident alone from the fact that Jesus obviously said and did considerably more than was written down in the earliest tradition. A complete account of his life was not attempted nor even possible. Only what was useful for preaching was passed along. We have no idea of his appearance, and apart from a few exceptions we are not able to date the events in his life. We cannot even state with any certainty the day of his death; the most we can do is conjecture that it was on Friday. The facts that were not transmitted were not deemed important by the church for its preaching. The selection of what was passed along was determined by the setting in life for the purpose of proclaiming a message, not presenting the past. Hence this oldest level of tradition is not a historical account, but a witness of faith; it is the apostolic testimony to Jesus.

Interpreted History

We should not conclude, however, that *everything* is uncertain. While it is true that we do have to rely upon the apostolic witness to Jesus—only in this sense could the church ever be an apostolic church—it is not necessarily an admission that we are dealing with uncertainties. This will become clear as soon as we see what role the faith of the witnesses played in the transmission of tradition.

The allegation that Jesus healed the sick should be considered historically valid. Which of the accounts of healing are historically "genuine" in their details cannot be given with confidence, but the fact that the oldest levels of tradition contain so many stories of healing is more easily explained by assuming that there actually were individual examples of healing which later attracted other healing accounts, than by assuming that all such stories are secondary formations.

The statement that "Jesus healed," however, only leaves us with a bare historical fact; establishing this does nothing more than say that there was such a historical fact. That he healed was not at all unusual for that day when healings were attributed to many individuals. The problem arises when we look past the bare statement that something actually occurred to the *meaning* of the fact. At this point a storm begins to brew.

The problem may be illustrated by recalling one of the controversial questions found in the Gospels: Are the demons cast out by the finger of God or by Beelzebul? (Luke 11:20). The question cannot be answered merely by stating that it is a fact—this is assumed! What is required is an interpretation and, with it, the taking of a position. The opponents who argued that Jesus cast out the demons by the devil had their viewpoint, those who insisted it was by the finger of God had another, completely opposite one. Both sides have claimed more than objective observation permits; both have made judgments of faith. The historical Jesus in his historical essence here is capable of being represented (as a historical phenomenon) in at least two or even more ways. Whether one position is correct and the other incorrect is not a judgment that can be made by historical methods. One sees in Jesus the words and works of God, the other takes him for a deceiver who should be destroyed. Both of these decisions of faith are based upon the same historical data.

We would gain nothing of any theological value if we tried to reach behind the kerygmatic witness to Jesus, as the revelation of God, with the historian's tools in order to find a pure historical picture. None exists anyway. Every human viewpoint implies some meaning, so that a pure historical picture is an artificial abstraction. By the very nature of the problem, then, it is justifiable, both historically and theologically, to take the apostolic witness to Jesus as the starting point. The historian could of course also include the Jewish polemic against Jesus in his study, but here, too, the problem of meaning or interpretation intrudes. In view of our knowledge of the sources, the historian in the last resort relies upon the apostolic witness to Jesus as the oldest source. The Christian attitude toward faith has always been to believe along with the (first) witnesses. If I want to reach behind the faith of the first witnesses, it means I am trying to give my faith historical certainty, but this, as we have already seen, is completely impossible. Furthermore, such an undergirded faith would no longer be faith since whatever I can ascertain historically no longer requires faith. When I try to support my faith historically, I do it to avoid the risk of faith.

It should again be clear that the program of the liberals was incorrect. They wanted to reach the undogmatic Jesus (the historical Jesus) by doing away with what they called embellishments. Their efforts were not successful because the facts they ended up with were simply abstractions which said nothing.

Form criticism shows that even the oldest level of tradition, far from being free of dogma, assigned meaning to Jesus in accordance with faith. We still have to define more precisely the exact nature of the "dogmatic elements" that are part of the picture of Jesus.

Bultmann's Objection

Rudolf Bultmann has consistently and emphatically maintained that we have no right to make any historical inquiry about what lay behind the kerygma. This should also be clear from what I have just said. But one point here should not be overlooked, as the example of the Bismarck anecdote will demonstrate. A nonhistorical anecdote may be "true" even though the details never actually happened. The decision as to whether it is true or not depends on whether it mirrors the actual or possible events in Bismarck's life. If, for instance, it pictures him as an ascetic, then regardless of how witty it may be, it definitely is not true.

In the same way the post-Easter preaching cannot be assumed to be theologically correct simply because it is a statement of faith about Jesus, behind which we are (supposedly) not allowed to inquire. The post-Easter kerygma can be said to present Jesus properly only if it stands up under examination, although not an examination consisting of a search for historical facts from the life of Jesus (Bultmann's great contribution has been to show that this is not possible). Instead, it has to be examined to determine whether it has a *direct* relationship with the earliest preaching about Jesus that still had some connection with the post-Easter Jesus.

It is important that the post-Easter proclamation be measured against the kerygma because the later preaching is a repetition of the earlier—in another language and with other concepts—yet is still dependent upon the earlier. It remains to be seen therefore whether the later kerygma is faithful to the subject matter, whether the subject matter has been preserved.

Summary: We have now modified somewhat what was said earlier by defining more exactly what I called the "beginning." At the close of the first chapter I said that the norm is the beginning and the beginning is Jesus.

But this we have now honed more precisely to mean the following: The beginning is not simply Jesus in his historical essence but is the direct apostolic witness to Jesus through faith.

THE APOSTOLIC WITNESS TO THE NORM

What did the apostolic witness to the norm look like? I must ask for your indulgence here. Thus far, as well as I could, I have tried to give reasons for everything I have said. But for what follows this will not always be possible. I want to show what the contents of the oldest kerygma were but in the space allotted I cannot give all the explicit reasons why it is the oldest. In order to do this, I would have to develop in detail the history of preaching in the period before the writing of the synoptic Gospels and this would mean justifying why one level of tradition is older, another not so old, accurately describing the criteria employed in making·these judgments, and so on. It should be obvious that this would easily exceed the limits of the theme of this book. Therefore I must restrict the discussion to just a few of the reasons. (In somewhat more detail I have set forth the grounds in my short book, *The Beginnings of Christology*, Fortress Press, 1969.)

Eschatology

The apostolic witness to Jesus in the oldest tradition is characterized by a well-marked eschatological thought. Throughout one finds a definite attitude toward the relationship to the end.

In Jesus' day the expectations for the future in Jewish hearts were determined by a movement in late Judaism called apocalypticism. During that period writings appeared which bear some similarity to the last book of the New Testament, the Revelation of John (the Greek title is the Apocalypse of John), and form a literary class of their own. A distinctive feature of Jewish apocalypses is an awareness of the imminence of the end, at least in the sense that it is possible to survey the time remaining until the end. A rather loose description of an apocalypse is that it provides a "timetable" of the last things and, related to this, a vivid portrayal of those last things. It also unfolds the events that are still to come before the end and describes what conditions will be like when it is all over. Part of their style is to pass off the authors as men of the past and, accordingly, the first section of an apocalypse contains descriptions of the past but is written in the form of prophecies of the future. In this way the men of the past are represented as seeing in advance the events that had taken place. If the reader then studies their accounts of the course of world history up to the present, it will become obvious to him that they were correct and should therefore be trusted when they speak of events still to happen.

The pictures of the future in the different apocalypses are by no means all identical. At times their outlook is particularistic, at times universal. The particularistic attitude shows itself, for example, in having the enemies of Israel destroyed while Israel itself enjoys salvation; the universal mood sees the Gentiles coming to Zion

from the ends of the earth and the God of Israel asserting himself and all who subject themselves to him
becoming members of the kingdom.

Another characteristic is their description of a great
judgment that occurs at the end. A number of different
figures play a role in this judgment, among them the
"Son of man." What is said about him also varies considerably: he is hidden, or he comes in the clouds or from
the sea, he is pictured as an advocate before the throne
of God, or at times as the judge himself, who pronounces
sentence in God's place and whose decisions are accepted
by God. The details of individual apocalyptic schemes
may differ, but the coming of the Son of man—however
it may be conceived—is nevertheless widespread.

In the Gospels Jesus is presented as the Son of man,
although not by direct testimony. Instead, Jesus speaks
of the Son of man as though he had in mind a third
person, and yet there is no doubt that he himself is
meant. When he announces his sufferings—the Son of
man will be scorned, mocked and killed, and after three
days resurrected—it is an unequivocal reference to himself as the Son of man. Or when he says that the Son of
man has no place to lay his head, it is also clear that he
is referring to himself.

It is extremely unlikely, however, that he ever considered himself to be or even identified himself with the
Son of man. This is supported by the evidence of the
unmistakable tendency of tradition to represent Jesus as
the Son of man even though this was not true of earlier
traditions (cf. Mark 8:27 with Matthew 16:13). In addi-

tion to this, there are two sayings about the Son of man in which Jesus has not yet been identified with the Son of man and in which, in fact, the distinction between the two personalities is clearly maintained: "And I tell you, every one who acknowledges me before men, the Son of man also will acknowledge before the angels of God, but he who denies me before men will be denied before the angels of God" (Luke 12:8–9); "For whoever is ashamed of me and of my words in this adulterous and sinful generation, of him will the Son of man also be ashamed, when he comes in the glory of his Father with the holy angels" (Mark 8:38). It is difficult to imagine that after Jesus had once been identified with the Son of man or had arrogated this to himself sayings could arise in which the identification has not been made explicit. A safe conclusion therefore is that the Son of man statements of Luke 12:8–9 and Mark 8:38 belong to the oldest level of tradition. From this we can say as a matter of historical judgment that Jesus himself did not equate himself with the Son of man.

How do we interpret these two Son of man sayings? Their depictions of the future are not quite identical. In the Gospel of Luke (that is, in the words passed along by Luke) the Son of man makes his acknowledgments *before the angels of God* who appear as the heavenly court or as the tribunal with the Son of man the advocate in the court. In Mark (that is, in the saying passed along by Mark), to the contrary, the Son of man comes *in the glory of his Father with the holy angels* and apparently is himself the judge. In spite of the disparate views of the future shown by the differences in details there is still a point of agreement. It is too superficial to say it is Jesus' announcement of the coming of the Son of man for that would mean his eyes are fixed on the future for which many differing interpretations would have been suggested. Furthermore, the ideas and concepts concerning the future are assumed to be known. The significance rather is found in this attitude: "You do not know how the Son of man will decide. You will face the tribunal, and you do not know how the judgment will fall. But I say to you: 'The judgment will depend upon your relationship to me now'." With this claim Jesus anticipates the future, for whoever receives his word now and follows him now need have no fear of the future; such a person already has the future, not in the shallow sense that he still has some time left, but rather has it as salvation. The future is no longer dark, uncertain, or threatening, but bright and is in fact salvation. And the decision for this is made by deciding now for Jesus.

With these words the early church declares: We have met Jesus in that we have established a relationship with him and our future is therefore secure. The fact that apocalyptic thought has been pushed off center here and the way this has been accomplished is immediately clear. Hans Conzelmann, the German New Testament scholar, has summarized this as follows: The question about the future as a question is dismissed with the *description* of the future now replaced by one's *attitude* toward it. The future people *knew about* has become one involving *faith*.

Another example may help here. We all know that we must die but the question is whether we *believe* it.

Especially as a young adult I may know this without the knowledge affecting my life or without my considering the implications. This can only mean I know it but do not believe it. Believing is not to be defined as taking a trip along a dark path that leads to facts not ordinarily accessible to the senses and then holding these facts to be true. A definition like this would fit apocalyptic works in which, by means of secret revelations, the writers were privy to a view of the future that was then upheld as true. Here something is known that otherwise cannot be known; but this has nothing to do with faith.

Our concept of "believing" is often murky, and because of this we tend to obscure its true theological meaning. To believe implies that one is undergirded in his existence, that he is aware of obligations in his life, in his deeds, in his thoughts. Hence it is misleading to drive a wedge between faith and action. The entire being of the person who believes is controlled by the object of his faith, and this results in concrete action. Activity does not somehow follow faith but is its expression; it is the incarnation of faith, and where it is missing, faith, too, is missing. Sin, then, is not to be construed as the transgression of a law or a commandment, but as the rejection of the possibility of the direct accessibility to God. It basically means that there is no exercise of faith when that possibility exists. What has traditionally been called sin are only symptoms, and we should never speak of sins (in the plural).

Therefore, the man who truly believes that he must die and does not simply know it as a fact will now draw out the implications; these will of course be different for different people. The one who tries to wrest as much from life as he possibly can because he must die believes in his own death because it determines his course. However, because he believes that his death spells the end, destruction, or extinction, his belief is also expressed as anxiety or dread.

In the Son of man sayings a different frame of mind is found. The future that people merely know about has become one requiring faith—in particular, faith that the future spells salvation. And because the witnesses experienced that Jesus had resolved the problem of the future in advance—viz., the future is salvation—their faith was relieved of all anxiety. The man who now believes in the future as salvation through Jesus need no longer be fearful, need no longer believe in his own death, although he is naturally aware that it will occur. Concisely expressed, it means that death has been conquered and robbed of its powers. At the same time it is clear that these are not objective statements, the only objective element here being the admission that death still retains its powers since I must die. But the one who believes in the future as salvation through Jesus does so, as it were, straight through and beyond death, because now in his faith he knows that his life is undergirded and therefore delivered from anxiety. In the framework of the Son of man sayings the usual *descriptions* (differing considerably) of the future are now replaced by a believing *attitude* toward the future as salvation. This was the experience of the witnesses in their encounter with Jesus as they trusted his words. And this they passed along by announcing his claims to others.

In Jewish thought about the future the end is also represented as a feast at the table of God, and for this reason even the simplest earthly meal had cultic overtones. This comes to expression in their prayers and ritualistic regulations on eating, to cite just two examples. Accordingly, a Jew would not eat with non-Jews or even with other Jews who were ritualistically unclean, a conviction still found among orthodox Jews today.

Jesus, on the other hand, welcomed the fellowship of tax collectors and sinners around the table, allowing outsiders to join in the ritual, since the meal was clearly cultic in character. He shattered the wall separating the pious from the godless and made a present reality out of something in Jewish thought that was not supposed to appear until after the judgment (despite the uncertainty about the exact time pious thinking was still assured it would occur). The early church joined in the experience and told the world that in its fellowship with Jesus it had already celebrated—and continued to celebrate—the meal reserved for the end time.

In many of the older accounts of healing a remarkable relationship exists between healing and faith. This is especially evident in the phrase which appears seven times in the synoptic Gospels: "It is your faith that has saved (or healed) you." A conspicuous feature is that faith is never said to be directed at Jesus, with the single exception of Matthew 18:6. (In Paul's writings and later in the Gospel of John the viewpoint is quite different.) It is also quite striking that in these older traditions Jesus ascribes faith to individuals—even Gentiles—without first requiring of them a confession of faith. As these people meet Jesus they are led into faith and, as they believe, allow to happen to them what only God can do. Nothing would be more indefensible than to understand all this as autosuggestion on the part of those healed. Rather, the events that take place here are all associated with Jesus who awakens in those in need a feeling of confidence that they can be helped. For God indeed does help, and afterward Jesus supplies the significance of what took place. Not until some of the later traditions on healing had developed was Jesus himself pictured as a miracle worker in accordance with the ideas of that day.

Earlier I said that in considering a healing it is not possible to ascertain whether God or the devil is at work. The interpretation, which transcends the mere statement of the fact as such, is very much a judgment based on faith. What the church saw in the deeds of Jesus was capable of a wide range of explanations. In one place it says that Jesus cast out demons by the finger of God (Luke 11:20). The same thought but in completely different terms occurs, for example, in the well-known inquiry of John the Baptist (Matt. 11:2–6) who asks through his messenger: "Are you he who is to come, or shall we look for another?" The question is concerned with the "kind" of person Jesus is (Who are you?) but the answer draws attention away from a possible description of his person and concentrates on what happens when one meets him: the blind receive their sight and the lame walk, lepers are cleansed, the deaf hear, the dead are raised up, and the poor have the "Gospel" preached to them. Herein lies the uniqueness of the answer.

Some commentaries take the position that the question of whether Jesus was the one who was supposed to come is not answered and the entire matter left hanging in the air. In one sense this is correct because it is not really answered, and apparently there was not supposed to be any answer to the question of who Jesus was. And yet it really is not ignored, for a response does follow which also sharpens the question at the same time. The reply— tell John what you see and hear: the blind receive their sight and the lame walk, lepers are cleansed, etc.— appears at first glance to be simply a report of something that happened. But it is phrased in the language of the Old Testament and becomes therefore not so much a report as a witness using Old Testament words, and in particular, Old Testament words with an eschatological ring. By their use an announcement is framed of what man can expect in the end time.

The answer thus directs attention away from the person to an event. But by employing Old Testament terms which are associated with the expectations of the end time, the event is given an eschatological interpretation, implying that through Jesus there has already occurred what was not actually expected until the last days. This, too, is a judgment based on faith. The interpretation, formulated in this case through the choice of language, is an affirmation that cannot be determined by objective study, yet only with this interpretation in mind is the admonition of Matthew 11:6 understandable: "And blessed is he who takes no offense at me." It would be puzzling if the paragraph (Matt. 11:2–6) merely referred to knowledge of what had taken place; but one could very easily be offended by the claim that with Jesus the end time has been ushered upon us.

The Working of God

It will be worth our while to examine this paragraph (Matt. 11:2–6) in more detail. The parallel passage in Luke 7:18–23 is instructive. There in verse 21 it says: "In that hour he [Jesus] cured many of diseases and plagues and evil spirits, and on many that were blind he bestowed sight." In Matthew this sentence is missing, and one wonders whether it was omitted by Matthew or added by Luke. We should notice first that immediately preceding this paragraph in Luke there is the account of the raising of the young man of Nain (Luke 7:11–17). By means of this story and the addition of verse 21 Luke is able to furnish proof that Jesus actually performed everything mentioned in his answer to John the Baptist. The same tendency is also present in Matthew. After the Sermon on the Mount he brings together miracle stories in chapters eight and nine as evidence for the details of the answer to John and he underscores this with the report in chapter ten of the mission of the disciples who preach the gospel to the poor! By the time the reader comes to Matthew 11:2–6 he knows that everything did happen just as Jesus had informed John the Baptist. Hence, Matthew, too, emphasizes that the events actually occurred as described. It is quite improbable, then, that Matthew omitted the addition of Luke 7:21, and more likely that it was first introduced into the tradition by Luke.

We know that the elements of tradition circulated in

independent units before their incorporation into the Gospels. According to the results we have arrived at up to this point, we have to distinguish between the individual unit of tradition and its reworking in the Gospels. Illustrative of this is the fact that Matthew 11:2–6, taken by itself, in no way emphasizes that all the actions listed in the answer actually occurred. Such a stress did not appear until the paragraph was worked into the context of the Gospel. Before that, the issue of whether they in actual fact took place was, strangely, not discussed.

It is curious therefore that the question of Jesus' identity receives no direct answer in the older tradition. As we have already seen, no answer was possible apart from faith. A neutral observer would not have been able to arrive at any conclusion since this requires taking a stand with regard to Jesus' deeds and knowing what they signify. Only by having allowed some work to be performed on him through Jesus could one experience who he was. Such an experience would also attest to its own character. If nothing had happened through Jesus, it would have been a matter of complete indifference to know who he actually was.

Let me put this in exaggerated form. It was not Jesus who was important but what he *did,* what he *brought,* what *event occurred* through him, what he *set in motion.* Nevertheless, what *he* did, what *he* brought, what *he* effected was also important but *he* was not important apart from his *deeds.* In short, the conviction of the first witnesses was: Jesus actualizes God. The immediate presence of God is made real by him. God is not a (temporally) distant God who only acts as judge at the end of the days, for Jesus makes real his coming *now*. Neither is he a (spatially) distant God reigning in the clouds, but One whose work (as in the healings) is made real *here* by Jesus. Through the deeds of Jesus the witnesses become aware that in his works the separation between God and man is eliminated. To the individual who enters into a relationship with him he makes God's presence a reality, and from then on nothing is allowed to come between God and him.

This gives us some insight into what has been called Jesus' "criticism of the law." Instead of scrapping it, he wanted men to do the will of God and not the law, because a codified law disrupts the direct relationship between God and man. Hence, even in this criticism his desire was that God "make himself near."

An apocryphal saying of Jesus in Luke 6:5 of the so-called codex D illustrates this point well: "On the same day he saw a man working on the Sabbath." Since this follows the paragraph on plucking corn on the Sabbath, one could easily assume that because of Jesus' critical attitude toward the Sabbath the man would be praised. But the saying continues: "Jesus said to him: 'Man! If you know what you are doing, you are blessed. But if you do not know, you are cursed and a transgressor of the law'." His criticism of the law is not offered just for the sake of criticism. If a man frees himself from formulated law, he simply puts himself in subjection to some other authority. It is possible to be disobedient to God even if the law is followed literally. The salient point in Jesus' thinking, however, is that a man should allow God to determine his manner of life. His criticism of the law cannot lead to libertinism, because in a more radical sense it binds one—to God.

Jesus' attitude with regard to the presence of God was this: He is not the God who is to come but the One who has already come. Not the distant, but the present God. Not the God who uses an intermediary, but the One who is directly accessible.

It would not be difficult to gather additional evidence which points in the same direction, but I want to stop here. The purpose of the oldest tradition, the apostolic tradition, was not to record facts from the life of Jesus, but to make clear and to bear witness to what happened through him. In their encounter with Jesus the witnesses became aware that they were being placed before God and were experiencing his nearness. God was not put at their disposal, but they did come to know his nearness as an event which Jesus "accomplished" for them. It is not the place here to establish why this is part of the oldest tradition, the apostolic (i.e., directly oriented on Jesus) kerygma, but by indirect evidence I can show why this is so.

In the Matthew 11:2-5 paragraph we saw that John's inquiry which focused on the character of Jesus' person was answered—quite contrary to the intention of the question—with a testimony of what Jesus had done. An interesting development appears if we differentiate between statements about the person of Jesus and descriptions of his works, that is, between the witness to Jesus and the witness to his *accomplishment*.

In the oldest sayings of the Son of man we have a witness to an accomplishment; Jesus anticipated the judgment of the Son of man with whom he was not identified. Through the description of an event here witness was borne to something important involving Jesus. Later, after reflecting upon the person of Jesus, Christians began to call him the Son of man. The evolution from the witness to the deed to the witness to Jesus himself is unmistakable, the emphasis no longer resting on what *happened* through Jesus, but now on what *he* could do. A similar development is found in the healing stories. I have already said that the oldest accounts of healing do not describe how Jesus healed. They simply report that healing occurred when Jesus called forth the faith that permitted God to work. Not until a later time was Jesus represented in healing stories as the one who himself was able to heal. In our traditions both ideas are occasionally found together with each pervading the other. It is interesting to observe, however, that with the passage of time the witness to the accomplishment diminished. I do not believe this was accidental. We can easily appreciate that while Christian believers were still close in time to an event itself, they would testify to it and to what it accomplished. Later, a particular event would still be described in a form acknowledging the accomplishment, but since it could never again occur after Good Friday, it is only natural that now the witness to Jesus' person would receive the greater stress whenever the event was described; this was done by showing how Jesus was able to heal. Paul's writings demonstrate this quite clearly. Having never seen Jesus, he says absolutely nothing about any earthly accomplishment of his in his preaching.

If we proceed backwards from this development (and this is what the historian does), it becomes plain that the testimonies to what was accomplished belong to an older age because they still highlight the works of the earthly Jesus.

This also explains why the earthly Jesus—as far as we can determine—never applied any of the christological titles (Christ, Son of man, Son of God) to himself—and why the question of who he was was never answered by the use of titles in the older traditions, reference being made instead to what he had done. Jesus was more concerned with others than with himself. It was not because he was the Christ that he brought God near; but because he brought God near he was called the Christ, the Son of man, and the Son of God. These christological ascriptions to Jesus resulted from the fact that Christians first turned over in their minds what had happened through Jesus and then stated explicitly who it was who brought this to fulfillment.

From these paragraphs we can conclude that it was a trait of the oldest tradition to make use of an event to show how God, temporally and spatially distant and separated from man by a written law, became a present reality through Jesus. I am omitting a detailed discussion of the contemporary ideas and concepts found in the older traditions except to remark that there was no attempt to harmonize them. The fact that they were left completely unharmonized suggests that they were in themselves apparently not the main concern. They were already a part of the world of ideas of that day and as such were pressed into service. But Christians felt no particular obligation toward them, otherwise there would have been some effort to bring them into agreement with each other. Instead, the most widely differing ideas and concepts were employed to speak of the immediate nearness of God.

My earlier question of whether the subject matter can ever be expressed is to be understood from this viewpoint. The subject matter is in fact always conditioned because the categories that must be used in discussing it are themselves products of their own time. What Jesus brought, however, was not a precise idea but the action of God. And yet, even this always had to be expressed in concepts (already in existence) with which each particular audience was familiar.

EASTER

At the beginning, we have said, there was the accomplishment, and not until a later time did Christian reflection begin to turn from the deed to the doer. The description of any event that bore witness to Jesus' role in setting in motion the working of God would naturally say something about him. As important as the working of God was in the oldest tradition, Jesus was never merely a secondary figure. But we must distinguish between this implicit Christology and the later explicit Christology that answered the question of who Jesus was by means of christological titles. The difference between the two is due to Easter, for beyond all doubt Easter was of absolutely fundamental importance for Christian faith after Good Friday. In our study we will have to give careful attention to just how far it was constitutive here. (In this connection the reader may wish to refer also to my book, *The Resurrection of Jesus of Nazareth,* Fortress Press, 1970.)

The main regard of the oldest kerygma was its witness to what Jesus accomplished, namely, the actualization of God. But Good Friday became a decisive turning point, for after Good Friday the event (the actualization of God) was no longer possible in the same form. After the death of Jesus it should really have been spoken of only as something in the past, perhaps along these lines: "In a blessed past, now unfortunately gone, it was possible for a person to experience the presence of God through Jesus." It is significant, however, that Jesus' act is not presented in this manner; it is not given as a historical report nor in the form of historical reminiscence, but as kerygma! The actualization of God still occurs even now in the kerygma despite Good Friday and is still related to Jesus.

There are a number of ways of trying to explain how this conviction could develop. The problem opens up a wide field for speculation, and we should not dwell on it here except to ask what reason was given by the early church itself. The church's response was that Jesus had been resurrected. Superficially at least, it means that Easter formed the bridge between Jesus and the early church. We should not be too easily satisfied with this explanation, however, and should ask to what extent Easter was this bridge.

There are two sides to the last question. First of all it asks about the factuality of the event. What actual occurrence lies behind the term "Easter" that we customarily explain with the word "resurrection"? And secondly, it asks about the quality and content of the statements associated with the event, so that with Good Friday a discontinuity was not introduced and the actualization of God could still be offered in the kerygma to anyone who desired to become involved.

A sharp distinction between the two parts of the question is not really possible. I said previously that the apprehension of a fact is inseparable from the process of determining its meaning, and the reduction of the apprehension of a fact to nothing more than the actual bare happening leaves an artificial abstraction. And yet in the case at point we should be careful to keep both aspects separate. For here the question about what actually happened often takes on a meaning that is not at all suitable to the discussion. Sometimes the suggestion is made that theological statements can be formed by stressing facts of an unusual nature. But if I state in strongest terms that the crucified one has been brought back to life and taken up into heaven, we have, it is true, an occurrence which is both miraculous and to our way of thinking very unusual, but which in no way demands the usual interpretation. The following inference is just as plausible: "God has acknowledged the one who was rejected by men. They were not worthy of him, and for this reason he was taken from them. Yet, they should at least know what they have lost, before they are left alone." In our present problem there is naturally a profound interest in what actually took place, but one should be mindful of the limits of historical inquiry. If we strip down the Easter events to the bare happening, we are left with only an abstraction that tells us nothing. Here as well, we cannot have facts without interpretation. Nevertheless, even though a fact is ultimately inseparable from the meaning it had for its witnesses, we should still try to inquire into what actually occurred, as far as this is feasible with the sources at our disposal.

The Historical Question

Occasionally the argument is put forth that the resurrection of Jesus was a reality beyond the scope of what can be known through historical investigation, and consequently the historical question is completely inappropriate here. Such reasoning is too simplistic, however, for at one time what we call the resurrection did have historical effects which, as such, are quite open to historical study. Or, are we not supposed to make any historical inquiries about first century Christianity or its origins? Against this view we merely need to recognize that the resurrection occupies a prominent place in the earliest Christian writings which are to be studied by historical means as historical documents. Admittedly, the reader derives from them only as much information about the resurrection as they bear witness to—and no more—but this does not support the assumption that historical inquiry is invalid here. The insights of form criticism in the interpretation of the texts on the resurrection are not to be slighted. However, there is a difference between drawing the conclusion on the basis of form criticism that the texts yield no data of a historical nature —this would have to be established anyway—and arguing that everything in the texts is to be understood in such a way that I can speak of a metahistorical reality which renders the historical method superfluous. Paradoxically, this very assertion cannot be made until the historical study of the texts has run its course!

What about the sources? The witness to Easter is found in two forms, one direct and one indirect, each fundamentally different from the other. The indirect witness, usually overlooked because Easter is not the theme —in fact, is not even mentioned—is lodged in the early synoptic tradition itself. For the continual preaching of the event accomplished by Jesus as kerygma after Good Friday has a solid basis of its own which distinguishes it from a mere recital of past events. We find little help in explaining this conviction by referring to Easter since this is just a word which by itself does not say very much. Nevertheless, the very fact that following Good Friday the tradition about Jesus was still being passed along is evidence of a certainty we usually identify by the term Easter.

The direct witness to Easter appears in three different forms.

A. It occurs in traditions containing detailed accounts of the appearance of the Resurrected One. They vary widely; Jesus not only shows himself to his disciples, but also walks, talks, and eats with them, passes through closed doors, etc.

B. The witness to Easter is also found in the traditions about the empty grave, and they, too, vary widely. In

one account three women are at the grave, in another
two. One report has a single angel appearing, another
two angels. According to one account the stone has
already been moved away by the time the women arrive
at the grave, but in another it happens before their eyes.
The tomb is guarded and it is not guarded. The women
go into the tomb or merely peer in. Peter is the first to
enter the tomb, although in the race toward it another
disciple arrived first.

C. Apart from the creedal statements in which the
Resurrected One or God's act in the resurrection is simply mentioned, there is a witness to Easter in short
formulas which speak of the Resurrected One as having
been seen. In this sense they are similar to the accounts
in group A, yet differ by asserting merely *that* he was
seen and give no further indication of the circumstances,
accompanying appearances or other events.

There is little doubt that the third group represents the
oldest form of the direct witness to Easter, especially
from a *literary* viewpoint. In 1 Corinthians 15:3–8 Paul
quotes an older tradition which, he says, he himself had
received: "For I delivered to you as of first importance
what I also received, that Christ died for our sins in
accordance with the scriptures, that he was buried, that
he was raised on the third day in accordance with the
scriptures, and that he appeared to [or, was seen by]
Cephas, then to the twelve. Then he appeared to more
than five hundred brethren at one time, most of whom
are still alive, though some have fallen asleep. Then he
appeared to James, then to all the apostles. Last of all, as
to one untimely born, he appeared also to me."

We need not take up in detail the problems this paragraph of Paul's raises except to mention two. We are not sure, for example, how much consists of the tradition Paul received and where he begins his own words. And the repetition of the lists of witnesses is remarkable: in one series Peter, the twelve, and the five hundred are named and in the other, James, all the apostles and then Paul. But Peter belongs to the twelve (which after Judas's death were really only eleven) and James should be counted with the apostles. What relationship do the twelve in the first list bear to the apostles in the second? The questions are many.

Important for our study is the claim that the Resurrected One had been seen; this is a very early witness. When the Corinthian church was founded around A.D. 50, Paul was already in possession of the tradition, so that it had to be current (in basic form) at least during the fourth decade.

Paul's usual reference to his having seen the Resurrected One is just a statement *that* he had seen him (e.g., 1 Cor. 9:1). At a later date, the Acts of the Apostles in quite a different vein adds three detailed reports of Paul's Damascus experience replete with visions and voices (Acts 9:22, 26) with each differing from the other in the particulars. From a literary viewpoint the oldest Easter witnesses are those that state merely *that* he was seen. Detailed accounts of appearances as well as stories of the empty tomb, on the other hand, come from witnesses to be dated much later, although this does not necessarily mean that in the context of the "history of tradition" their traditions must also be considered later.

It is very possible that traditions which became fixed in written form at a later period reach quite far back in time. For this reason therefore we cannot yet draw any final conclusions on the basis of our study.

I have already called attention to the wide diversity among the reports of the appearances and the stories of the empty tomb. The details are recorded with such variety that harmonization is impossible. The coherent frameworks appearing in the Gospels are the result of the working together of these differing traditions by each Gospel writer. No Gospel reads exactly the same as another. The task of reconstructing an accurate sequence of events from these diverse accounts is therefore hopeless.

When the individual stories are studied more closely, a rather clear picture of the tendency of the tradition develops, namely, later tradition always becomes "more massive." If the earliest tradition merely speaks of seeing the Resurrected One, a somewhat later tradition informs us that he carried on conversations, while still later traditions announce that he passed through closed doors, ate with his disciples, allowed himself to be touched, etc. Such a tendency is understandable because the vivid certainty of the resurrection was preserved precisely by these additions. To prevent the disappearance of this reality, the aspect of seeing was constantly described in ever more realistic terms.

In line with these observations 1 Corinthians 15:3 ff. turns out to be the oldest tradition both in terms of the date of its composition and in the history of the traditions. The Greek word *ōpthē* is used here and may be translated as: He appeared, he allowed himself to be seen, or, he was seen. But this oldest tradition gives no inkling about the kind of seeing involved or about the circumstances surrounding it, and we are left in the dark.

Can we conclude anything about the actual happening hidden behind the term Easter? This much historical fact we may be sure of: several people claim to have seen Jesus after Good Friday. Peter was most likely the first, but beyond this we are uncertain of the order of those who followed. We are not able to reach behind the affirmation "we have seen him." It will not be worth the effort to try to overstep this historical limit by speculating in order to determine what first occurred that enabled the disciples to see Jesus. We must always keep in mind that the kerygma gives no information about this; the most we learn from it is how this seeing was interpreted.

A man was seen who was known to have died on a cross. That he was raised up or awakened from the dead is a conclusion drawn from the experience of seeing. At this point a clear distinction is necessary between what comes first and what comes second. In Aristotelian thought one must differentiate sharply between what is "first according to nature" and what is "first for us." In our study "first for us" is the seeing, and from this comes the conclusion about the "first according to nature," namely, "God raised him up." The order may not be reversed by beginning with a discussion or a description or anything of the sort of what is "first according to nature" with the hope of deriving information about the seeing. The actual process of the resurrection is neither described nor depicted (apart from several later post-

New Testament traditions); instead, the kerygma testifies to it (and in this way reveals it to us) on the basis of the seeing. The decisive point here is that the one who was crucified had been seen. Those who saw him were understandably not interested in emphasizing that they had beheld a miracle. They had undergone an experience from which they concluded: "He is not still among the dead, and therefore what he brought continues with us." With this assurance grounded in their Easter experience, they could begin to "pass along tradition." And this act at the first took the form of declaring the traditions about Jesus as kerygma (and not as historical reminiscence).

Easter at that time did not constitute a theme by itself. This explains why it is not mentioned in the oldest traditions about Jesus. It was experienced as the act which initiated the preaching after Good Friday. At first, no thought was given to it as an initiatory act, as Christians simply allowed themselves to be motivated by it. And this is why, as I have already said, the *That* of the kerygma (i.e., the fact that the tradition about Jesus was passed along) is the first, albeit indirect, witness to Easter.

Bultmann has made the following (very extreme) statement on the subject: Jesus was resurrected into the kerygma. There is no objection to this, as long as it is clear in our minds that his words do not refer to what I have called the initiatory act, but to what happened as a result of this act. In order to avoid misunderstandings it may be wiser not to say that he was resurrected into the kerygma but that he is present or lives in it, so that to be involved with the kerygma is to be involved with

him in a real sense. This marks out the difference between kerygma and a historical report. If the tradition
about Jesus were a historical report, we would have at
hand the thoughts, sayings, and deeds of someone in the
past. But if the kerygma confronts me, then someone living touches me who makes demands upon me now.

A common expression of dissatisfaction with this view
is that this cannot be all there is to it; there must be
more! Does it not diminish Easter or, for all practical
purposes, eliminate it? The objections, however, do not
hold up. The initiatory act, it is true, is no longer described as such, but in no place in the New Testament
tradition is this attempted anyway! In probing into the
past we simply cannot reach behind the fact that men
said that after the crucifixion they had seen the one who
had been crucified. The complaint that viewing the
problem in this light excludes the exercising of faith (vis-
à-vis historical events immediately following the crucifixion) can also be dismissed, since the resurrection,
which here provides the interpretation for the act of
seeing Jesus, is, as a recurring idea in the history of religions in general, not itself an object of faith. As a historical event, Easter is much more the act by which the
process of activating faith is set in motion. It is this—the
arousing of faith, or the activity of God—that Jesus
brought. In short, Easter is the instrument which sets in
motion the working of God after Good Friday. Such a
view hardly diminishes Easter! I must issue a plain warn-
ing here not to desire more than this. Otherwise it would
be an attempt to make faith certain. Faith, however, first
plays a role when—and only when!—I am asked whether

I will allow myself to be confronted with a message as a reality that makes claims upon me, or whether I see in the message simply the historical remembrance of someone long dead.

This recalls an earlier statement. I said that Jesus did not set into motion the working of God because he was the Messiah, but rather because of this he was called the Messiah. The much debated question about his messianic consciousness is a purely historical one. No theological question can be hewn from it because the obedience required by faith would then be dependent upon whether Jesus understood himself as the Messiah or not. And faith would not rest upon his word—such a risk would be genuine faith—but upon our own firm estimate of his character and would no longer constitute a risk. Quite apart from this, I would have gained nothing by ascertaining what his self-awareness (or self-understanding) was, for I would still have to decide whether I wanted to accept what he said and thought about himself; and if my decision were affirmative, why such a choice? My reasons would still only be based upon the conviction that he set into motion the working of God. A statement about oneself can, after all, be either true or false! In the same sense a prior belief that Jesus actually rose from the dead cannot be the basis for involving myself with the message. Quite the contrary. When I sincerely come face-to-face with the kerygma and entrust myself to it, I gain the certainty that he lives—but only then.

Belief in the resurrection of Jesus is to be implied only of the person who takes the kerygma seriously *today*.

The resurrection becomes a reality touching my life only as I meet and yield to the Jesus encountered in the kerygma, for there is no other place where one can meet him today.

The context of our discussion should make it immediately obvious that if Jesus is present in the kerygma, the kerygma must have something to do with Jesus. For the critical point in the Easter witness is the identification of the one who was seen with the one who had previously been with his people. Since Easter the old theme—not something new or different—has continued to be proclaimed. If it were no longer the old theme, it would also not be possible to speak of the identification of the one who was resurrected with the one who had formerly been among them. Hence the problem of Easter brings up the same point I mentioned in the first chapter of the book, although there from a completely different perspective, namely, Jesus is the norm for the later proclamation of the church.

Nothing less than Jesus himself is at stake here. The reason for this is that later preaching sounds very different from what I have called the apostolic witness of the norm and have summarized above.

I said that Easter is essential to Christian faith, but (as I added) one would have to ask to what extent this is true. The answer, I think, is found in a statement by Professor Ernst Käsemann: Easter has turned the *Once* into a *Once-For-All-Time*. It has made it possible to proclaim the events associated with Jesus without the necessity of his bodily presence. Easter's importance does not lie in its provision of something categorically new, an addition to what we already believe, but in the fact that without it there would have been no Christian faith after Good Friday. When Paul says, "If Christ has not been raised, your faith is futile and you are still in your sins" (1 Cor. 15:17), he is correct since without Easter the events of Jesus would have been lost in the mists of the past. But because of the identification of the Resurrected One with the one who had lived on earth, we are not offered something new, but what was brought by Jesus. And this takes place in the kerygma about Jesus, about which we spoke in the last section.

I repeat: Later preaching looks different from the apostolic witness to the norm, as sketched above. Thus the question is raised whether the subject matter or theme, so central to that apostolic witness, has been preserved.

Reflection

Several times in our discussion the thought has come up that later reflection tried to make clear what was implicitly stated about Jesus in the older traditions by means of their description of some event. As we look into the subject of Christology, we will differentiate between what was explicit and what was implicit. Early Christian proclamation, whose witness consisted solely of descriptions of what happened, tried to make clear by its mode of description what the witnesses experienced in their encounter with Jesus. But by keeping its focus on the event accomplished by Jesus its mode of description is basically different from the later explicit Christology. Even, for example, when Jesus is pictured in later healing stories as one who is able to heal, this kind of Christology is still to be distinguished from one in which titles (already at hand) are ascribed to Jesus. Two different attitudes are represented here, and we should be careful to observe the distinction. In the one, attention centers on an event which Jesus brings about, and in the other, he is himself the object of reflection. That he is the object is due, understandably, to his role as the one through whom God performed his work on the witnesses. To this degree the explicit Christology is an extension of an implicit Christology.

The tendency of the process of reflection can be explained by considering again the event accomplished by Jesus. We said that Jesus made God an actual reality so that through him men experienced the presence of God. As with the observation of any event, so here, the event accomplished by Jesus is given with an interpretation. The interpretation is not independent of the observer of the event. As we noticed, it was possible to see in the deeds of Jesus the work of God as well as the work of the devil, but the language of the event here is one. This is not the place to argue whether the language of events can be misunderstood, and if so, why. Of importance to us here is simply the fact that even an event has a language character. The event for which Jesus was responsible also has in this sense a language character which does not require the actual use of words for what is being communicated. To say that something has a language character does not mean that it must be expressed in words. When someone shows that he loves me by his conduct, actions, behavior, or attitude, his conduct has a language character without anything being said or the word "love" even being mentioned. The immediacy of the event renders actual speaking unnecessary; words could, in fact, even disturb the relationship by taking the edge off this direct contact.

Nevertheless, this event which speaks without words has to depend upon them whenever communication is desired with someone who was not a direct witness of the event. In recording the essence of the event with words, the description can either be as clear as possible so that the listener can draw for himself the meaning of the event, or it can be presented with a definite interpretation. To stay with our example: The behavior of my friend can either be described in a straightforward manner, or the actual word "love" can be used.

In the discussion of form criticism I said that an event was described so as to fulfill the purpose of the writer. We can now apply the principle. The description of the event associated with Jesus (i.e., the description of the event accomplished by him) has been recorded in such a way that it is not merely a report of something in the past but becomes a renewed message for the listener. Hence the past is set forth as kerygma.

The simplest form of reflection is the verbal description of an event as kerygma. Since this has to do with stories about Jesus, I am calling this form the Jesus-kerygma. As the process of reflection progressed, the event was not only given verbal expression, but explicit statements were also added about the person who was responsible for the event, and Jesus was soon identified in specific terms. Since this was done by ascribing christological titles to him, the most frequent of which was the name Christ, I am calling this the Christ-kerygma in distinction to the Jesus-kerygma.

The Son of man title, for example, was applied to Jesus in this way. Because the final judgment took place ahead of schedule as a result of one's relationship to Jesus, the eschatology of the event was accentuated by calling Jesus the Son of man. Through him there occurred what men thought would only be effected by the Son of man. And this prompted them to state the principle, as in Mark 2:10, for example, that as the Son of man Jesus had the power to forgive sins on earth. The places in the Gospel tradition where Jesus is described as *kyrios* (Lord) or as the Christ or Son of God belong to the same category.

The only remarkable aspect about this is that such predicates of Jesus are found relatively infrequently in the synoptics. Even though majestic christological titles have been introduced to the tradition about Jesus, the emphasis is still upon the description of the event accomplished by him. There was a certain danger here, however. In Easter men experienced that the working of God, instead of ceasing on Good Friday, could continue because Jesus did not remain among the dead. As a result of their past experience that Jesus brought God near, it would have been possible to express this as some kind of a general truth, although one could then no longer have said: Jesus brings God near. He could only have said: The possibility exists that God is present, as Jesus pointed out to us by his example. And this would have turned Jesus into the founder of a religion that continued to be practiced after his death. They had these alternatives: either, Jesus teaches that there is a new possibility, or, he makes the presence of God a reality. As a result of its Easter experience the primitive church chose the second proposition, namely, Jesus not only teaches that there is a new possibility, but he makes it real as well. During his lifetime this was all related to Jesus himself. Yet, after Easter it was still related to him because of the identification of the Resurrected One with the earthly Jesus. In order to maintain this and at the same time to underscore it firmly, Jesus was described in ever more explicit terms. This expanded description was ultimately a reflection upon the Easter experience, giving rise to an interpretation using such phrases as "he was seen," "he appeared," or "he lives."

The tradition about Jesus—at least as far as its formulation is concerned—is therefore unhistorical because he himself never made use of these titles. This interpretation of Jesus is nevertheless closely related to what he brought and concerned himself with during his life. In fact, it is by means of this very interpretation that his original concerns are kept intact.

We must bear in mind that these qualifications of Jesus' person are legitimate only to the degree that they express in words what his unique contribution was. The Son of man title, for example, brings together a wealth of ideas from the Old Testament and the apocalypticism of late Judaism. Within this variety one view of the Son of man represents him as a preexistent heavenly being who was with God before creation, then kept concealed, but whose role at the end of the world is described in a number of ways. Thus it would be wrong to ascribe such a complex of ideas to Jesus simply because someone has given him the title, Son of man. The first question always has to be: What was the main concern of Jesus? And the second has to be: *To what extent* was it possible to express this concern by applying to him concepts already current in the ancient world? The answer to this determines what "sector" of these concepts may be legitimately used when he is called the Son of man.

The titles of Jesus are predicates which call attention to the work of God through him and are allowable only insofar as they are able to do that. After his death the event accomplished by Jesus could of course no longer be directly described; Jesus himself became the object of reflection, and the predicate became a description of that event in a veiled form. In order to understand the affirmations about Jesus properly, it is necessary to work backwards from this veiled interpretation. Therefore, the title of Son of man, for example, when associated with Jesus, cannot be made to say or mean anything more than what was involved in the event itself.

This can be clearly seen by considering another area of the process of reflection. I have already spoken of the (still relatively infrequent) mention of Christology in the synoptic material, that is, the tradition about Jesus. We should now distinguish among three forms of the kerygma. There is, first of all, a pure kerygma about Jesus which is exclusively concerned with his *acts* and *words*. A second form, a mixture of the Jesus-kerygma and the Christ-kerygma, speaks of *Jesus Christ*. And there is a third form, the Christ-kerygma, in which the tradition about Jesus as such does not appear at all. Yet even here declarations about the person of Jesus are still expressions of the activity of God, although they are legitimate only in the measure that they actually can do this.

Let me show this by referring to the title "Son of God." From the viewpoint of the history of religions the expression has a dual background, one in Judaism and one in Hellenism.

In Judaism the (anointed) king, the people, and occasionally even the Messiah can be called the Son of God. They become a Son of God through the legal relationship of adoption. This thought is at the heart of the story of Jesus' baptism: "Thou art my beloved Son" (Mark 1:11). In the call of the voice from heaven after the baptism by John, the adoption formula of Psalm 2 is clearly in mind. (This account of the baptism of Jesus belongs to the Jesus-tradition, but is itself Christ-kerygma, for there is nothing here about the words and works of Jesus. This is also true of the story of the transfiguration, Peter's confession at Caesarea Philippi, and the narratives of Jesus' birth and childhood. In these accounts Jesus is occasionally referred to as the Christ when the description draws attention to what happened through and within him.)

In Hellenism Son of God is not a legal, but a "physical" title, expressing a physical relationship to the godhead. The Son of God has a "divine nature" received either through miraculous procreation by means of the spirit without a human father, or through a direct act of procreation between a god and a human mother. For a Jew (then as now) this idea is unacceptable because in his eyes it brings divine majesty down to a human level. For this reason the thought first appears in the New Testament in the birth stories and other traditions which can be traced back to Hellenistic Christianity.

When the question is then asked whether Jesus was the Son of God, it cannot be answered until we know what is to be understood by the term Son of God. It is no help to turn to the New Testament because both thoughts cancel each other out. Therefore we have to indicate clearly which viewpoint we have in mind: Is the reference to the Jewish attitude, the Hellenistic, or something else?

Where does this leave us? By now it should be clear that we cannot simply take the idea as it stood and apply it to Jesus. Let me also stress this—for the third time: The affirmations about Jesus are statements about the activity of God through him and are legitimate only to the extent that they express such activity through him. The concept Son of God, then, as it occurs in the post-Easter Christ-kerygma and is applied to Jesus, must be interpreted from the viewpoint of what happened through Jesus. Jesus (subject) is the Son of God (predicate). This predicate cannot be made to say anything more than what is to be implied from the event accomplished by Jesus. The term Son of God includes a good many other ideas, in Judaism as well as in Hellenism, but since they are inappropriate for describing what occurred through Jesus, they may not be read into the predicate. The question of whether adoption or procreation through the Spirit was intended is of no consequence here, the only important observation being that the event accomplished by Jesus brought man into contact with God. The purpose of the term Son of God is to declare that he who accomplished it was extremely close to God.

The concepts and ideas of both Judaism and Hellenism are theologically acceptable only insofar as they express the main concerns of Jesus' life. From the Jewish viewpoint it was quite acceptable to call Jesus the Son of God if the intention was to declare that he set in motion the working of God. From the Hellenistic viewpoint it was also correct for the same reason. The phrase in both cases includes other widely varying ideas which do not concern us here. We can understand them, but only in a historical sense, since Son of God is an idea that has become foreign to us.

We must be careful here. If a title is ascribed to Jesus to make it clear who it is who brings God near, each particular idea associated with the title can very easily assume an independent position of its own and operate as such. The Jew, for example, asked: "Since one becomes a Son of God through adoption, *when* did this occur in Jesus' life?" And this gave rise to the baptism tradition in Jewish Christianity that at the beginning of his public ministry he was adopted by God. (The baptism of Jesus by John can be accepted as historical fact. The very early church would never have invented the account, for the tradition shows clearly that the dependence of Jesus upon the Baptist in the baptism was considered a problem to which quite diverse solutions were offered. One possibility was to say that with the anointing after the baptism the adoption by God was completed. Thus from the time of his baptism Jesus was the Son of God.) On the other hand, in Hellenistic circles the question was asked: "Since the Son of God is a physical offspring of God, *how* did this take place?" This in turn produced the birth narratives.

In each instance reflection began with what Jesus accomplished. It centered upon the one whose own deeds set God's work in motion and by means of the concept of Son of God expressed his nearness to God. But the idea it conjured up in Jewish thought was quite different from that of Hellenistic thought. Each existed independently of the other and encouraged the introduction of additional notions which went far beyond the original intent. We saw this in the baptism tradition and in the birth narratives. (When I speak here of the birth stories, I do not have in mind primarily the well-known Christmas story of Luke 2 which says nothing of a miraculous birth. I am referring to the birth announcement to Mary in Luke 1 or the birth story in Matthew. Luke 2 belongs to the Christ-kerygma but the miraculous element is not the birth but the fact that the newborn baby was proclaimed *soter* [Saviour] by the angels!)

The process of reflection in the Easter traditions proceeded in a very similar fashion. Those who saw Jesus after Good Friday began to announce this, but at the same time turned the matter over in their minds: If we have seen him, then he has been brought back from the dead, and we can represent him as resurrected. And so a number of detailed accounts of his appearances were developed—harmonization is out of the question—to uphold the reality of the experience that motivated their preaching.

In time these individual accounts were included in the Gospels, and as soon as they were, the development reversed itself. Reflection always looks backwards; one moves from the event to the person who accomplished the event in order to think about his origins. As the Gospels present the case, however, what was originally the final element in the train of reflection now appears as the first. And right here there is a considerable danger.

We should always try to determine the direction in which interpretations have developed and then understand them in that light; in fact, we can use them only if we are aware of the direction. The purpose of the predicates of Jesus is to elucidate who it is who makes the presence of God so real; but if I reverse the direction, I turn that interpretation into a description and I make something absolute that the reflection has utilized for its interpretation. It is then no longer a question of whether and to what degree the interpretation still sheds some light on the event, since the interpretation itself is now considered to be a valid description of Jesus, from which one immediately reaches the event through deduction. The presentation of the birth stories in the Gospels is an example of this. They have been written in the form of historical accounts, given an absolute quality that makes them appear as valid descriptions, and placed at the beginning. Not until much later in the sequence of descriptions does the event accomplished by Jesus appear.

The same process of writing something down as history and reversing the direction occurs with the Easter traditions. The final conclusion of the disciples' reflection upon this experience was that Jesus was resurrected. From this they reasoned on the basis of Jewish anthropology that the grave must have been empty. Thus even the empty grave is a (late) interpretation resting upon the experiences of the disciples. But these last two interpretations, even though they are part of the secondary historical writing of the Gospels, appear there as primary history, that is, as descriptions. Then by proceeding from this description one is able to arrive at the event, the beginning of preaching after Good Friday. However, the experience of seeing Jesus which launched the preaching was, as we have seen, originally the point of departure for the reflection. The reversal of direction through a secondary historical presentation in the Gospels is especially evident here.

Reflection resulted not only in a qualifying of the person of Jesus, but also of his fate. The statements about the cross illustrate this most clearly. They can be divided into two groups. One group considers the cross as an event bringing salvation, the other speaks of the way of Jesus to the cross and the way of the cross to discipleship. Both, obviously, are related, although this cannot be shown very easily nor very quickly.

I will confine my remarks to the statements about the cross as an event of salvation. In the New Testament they are found in the Gospel of John and in Paul's writings, but never, or almost never, in the synoptic Gospels. This is remarkable, because according to traditional thought the decisive Christian declaration has to do with what happened on Good Friday. It is no exaggeration to say that the Protestant church regards Good Friday as its highest holy day. We should also add that this high esteem for the cross is true of Christians in general. It is the symbol of Christianity because it is "the place of salvation," or at least this is how it is understood.

The synoptic Gospels (the sources which bring us closest to the historical Jesus with the aid of form criticism), however, do not associate the cross with salvation. One could object that there is a passion narrative (Mark 14:1–15:47, for example) which shows that the Gospels (I am expressing this quite simply) represent the way of Jesus as the way to the cross, that is, the cross was his goal. Such an impression could only arise because the earliest individual parts of tradition were arranged in chronological order, even though they originally existed as independent units of kerygma each complete in itself. If they are brought together, it is quite understandable that the passion narrative will constitute the final phase of Jesus' "life." If the individual units are studied by themselves, however, they in no way point to the cross. This orientation (toward the cross) is the work of the evangelists who, as editors, set the material in sequence. A point worth noticing is that the so-called Q source which we can reconstruct from Matthew and Luke with some degree of certainty very likely knew nothing of a passion narrative nor of any Easter stories. We can conclude from this that the preaching about Jesus after Easter never mentioned the cross.

Earlier I drew attention to the fact that even the Gospel of Mark made use of sources already at hand, the most extensive of which was most likely a passion story. The Gospel was then put together by an editor who placed the other traditions he wanted to include before this passion story. If we now consider this "direction" in which the Gospel arose, it becomes evident that the trend of thought is not toward the cross but away from it. This holds true not only for the editing of the Gospel, whose editor—after Easter—could not very well disregard the church's experiences following the appearance of Jesus—regardless of how he used these in his work—but is especially true of the individual traditions. The announcements of Jesus' sufferings bear this out. As they presently stand, they point toward the cross, but originally they arose in a direction away from the cross. That is, after the events occurred, the words were put in Jesus' mouth as prophecies. (This principle has long been recognized in historical research and is called *vaticinia ex eventu*, prophecy after the event.)

In the synoptic Gospels the cross is not once described as a salvation event. The way of Jesus seemingly points toward the cross but this is due to secondary historicizing which has arranged the accounts in a certain sequence. Two statements about the cross as a salvation event admittedly do lend unmistakable support to such an arrangement: Mark 14:24 (and parallels) on the cup at the Last Supper and Mark 10:45 (and parallels) which speaks of a *lytron* (ransom). The latter passage reads: "For the Son of man also came not to be served but to serve, and to give his life as a ransom for many." It can be shown, however, that both of these interpretations of Jesus' death as an event of salvation are relatively late in comparison with the synoptic tradition as a whole. The *lytron* saying is a secondary expansion of the words about serving and does not fit in there, as a comparison of Mark 10:42–45 with Luke 22:24–27 plainly bears out. The statement on the cup of wine at the Last Supper is a result of the Hellenistic transformation of that tradition. I cannot discuss this problem in any more detail here, but I have covered it in my little book, *The Lord's Supper as a Christological Problem,* Fortress Press, 1970.

The cross as a salvation event first appears in later traditions, not in those which bring us closest to Jesus. If this is so, we can only conclude that Jesus himself did not understand his death as a salvation event. The direct witnesses of Jesus, at any rate, did not understand him as orienting his deeds and life toward the cross.

I am aware that this conclusion is shocking, or at least can have such an effect, because the cross as a salvation event has become an integral part of our faith. However, whether or not Jesus understood his death in this light is a purely historical question that must be answered not by my faith but through historical investigation. Caution! The historical question here is not whether the cross was in actual fact a salvation event but whether Jesus understood it as such, and this can only be answered historically. Whether the result of such inquiry determines what I am to believe or the extent to which my faith is affected is a matter to be worked out. But faith itself plays no role in the search for an answer.

It is now obvious that when we compare the apostolic witness to the norm, as we presented it above, with the preaching of the cross as a salvation event, we find tensions, to say nothing of contradictions. Setting the work of God in motion, kindling faith, celebration of the end time meal, and the attitude toward the final judgment—

all are related to the present. Jesus makes salvation available *now* and does not hedge it with the condition that he must first die. He says: "Your sins are forgiven you," not, "Because my cross will make the forgiveness of sins possible, I now (in view of this event) forgive your sins."

Not only the negative findings in the earliest strata of the synoptic tradition indicate that Jesus did not understand his death as bringing salvation, but the descriptions of his work as oriented toward the present time support this view as well. One can therefore no longer avoid the historical conclusion that Jesus did not view his death as a salvation event.

Does this not put us into a theologically embarrassing position? We have said that it is necessary to examine the later kerygma to see if it is still properly related to Jesus. For, as we see it, the central preaching of Good Friday faces us with an apparently unbridgeable gap, and we have to ask whether the preaching of the cross as a salvation event is false or theologically incorrect.

It is not out of order to inquire once more about how and where this preaching arose and—this is especially important—in which direction it arose. We can easily understand that the disciples were at a loss on Good Friday (although this would be difficult to understand if Jesus had attached some meaning to his death beforehand and had predicted a resurrection immediately after his death). Their perplexity and helplessness were not the result of any lack of knowledge of what his death signified; for them it represented a crisis of faith. If the disciples believed that they had experienced the working of God through Jesus, then his death could only have meant that they had been mistaken. Now, however, after Good Friday they see the one who had been crucified and experience that he lives! And they begin to preach. But what are they to think of the cross?

The interpretation of the cross in terms of salvation is conveyed in Paul's writings by the use of the so-called *huper* (for, on behalf of) phrases: for our sins, for us, for you, etc. These expressions (as well as later developments upon them) reveal that traditional ideas have been used which were already known and common in Judaism, as, for example, the thought of a vicarious sacrifice and of an offering for atonement.

According to the history of religions in antiquity it was widely held that animal sacrifices were offered to the god (or gods) to take care of the guilt of men and reconcile them with deity. Judaism was acquainted with the additional concept that a righteous man could suffer vicariously for the people and by his sacrifice effect atonement and reconciliation with God.

This idea was then applied to Jesus. As he set in motion the work of God by the accomplishment of the event, he steered men back to God, brought about reconciliation, forgave sins, etc. It was this very experience of the witnesses throughout the days of his active working that was then interpreted in terms of the cross, which became the last of his "deeds." Interpreting the cross as a salvation event was therefore a summary of the interpretation of all his works, which was then "localized" at one point in his life, the cross.

The point in Jesus' life where this summary is applicable is, however, interchangeable. In Galatians 4:4–5 one reads: "But when the time had fully come, God sent forth his Son, born of woman, born [or, set] under the law, to redeem those who were under the law, so that we might receive adoption as sons." When Paul continues: "And because you *are* sons," it becomes clear that what is said here of the coming of the Son of God—without the usual words, to be sure—is what is otherwise (and most frequently) associated with Jesus' death. Luther writes: "Today [that is, at Christmas] he is once again at the gate to the idyllic Paradise; the cherub no longer stands guard before it; praise, honor, and glory to God." These are statements which were formulated after Easter with reference to the work of Jesus, which emphasize what actually happened in his works, and which summarize it by focusing on Good Friday or Christmas.

If the interpretations did develop in this direction, then under no circumstances may the direction be reversed. If the direction were reversed, we would again be forcing later (confessional) statements to serve as firsthand accounts and we would be aiming at two points in time and would have to say that the reopening of Paradise, our reconciliation, occurred at Christmas *and* at Easter. The question, of course, is when did this really take place? If redemption was effected by Jesus' coming, then his deeds, and above all his cross, would be superfluous. If redemption was first made possible by the cross, however, then Jesus in performing his works would only be marking time until he died. It is only when the direction is reversed in this way that such opposing and completely unreconcilable views emerge.

The previous example also pointed this out. When Jesus is called the Son of God, both Jewish and Hellenistic thought add a number of ideas that were not originally intended. But if this designation of Jesus does not maintain a correct relationship to the event it is trying to illuminate, one may be led to ask when and how he was and became God's Son. Furthermore, it will be impossible to harmonize the Jewish idea of adoption with the physical notion of Hellenism. In the history of dogma a point was reached when a Christology based upon adoption was rejected (perhaps the dogma was flourishing in Hellenistic soil). But the problem could only have arisen in the first place because the direction in which the interpretations developed was no longer observed, and it was thought that it could be reversed.

Summary: At the end of the first chapter the New Testament was characterized as the oldest extant volume of preaching of the church. We disregarded the traditional attitude toward the canon and introduced the question about the norm. We have discovered that this norm is mediated to us in the apostolic witness as it describes an event accomplished by Jesus; we also found it in the form of reflection which presents the event in a somewhat veiled form. Such a veiled account must always be true to what was of central concern in Jesus' words and works. This was carried out both by qualifying the person of Jesus and through a summary of what actually happened in his work which was then interpreted in terms of his fate.

3.

The New

Accomplishment

In the treatment of the theme "The New Testament as the Church's Book" the idea of the "church" has appeared thus far only as a historical concept, in that we have spoken of the history of the church. In the first chapter especially the "ancient church" was frequently at the center of the discussion.

ECCLESIOLOGICAL PERSPECTIVES

The theme also has a present-day reference, however, and, as such, leads us to inquire about the church today. It is not my intention—nor is there room for it here—to develop an ecclesiology, a doctrine of the church. Nevertheless, I have a few thoughts for us to consider which, I think, grow out of all the previous discussion and which point up the relevance of that discussion for the present church.

The Two Possibilities

In our study it has been important for us always to keep in sight the event accomplished by Jesus to which

later reflection or interpretation attached itself. I have
been speaking not merely of one event, but of one event
accomplished by Jesus. This was to hold firmly to the
fact. that in the presentation of the apostolic witness of
Jesus the important point was always that God was
actively working and that this event was related to
Jesus. When I now use the abbreviated phrase "accomplishment of Jesus," the full meaning is still implied.

If it is true that the purpose of the reflection of the
apostles was to keep alive the memory of what took
place through Jesus and if reflection began with the
accomplishment and from this viewpoint described the
one responsible for it, then for the new accomplishment,
toward which the reflection is directed, there are two
possibilities. First, reflection upon the accomplishment
can completely conceal the accomplishment itself by
describing it in cryptic or veiled language with the result that the original purpose of the reflection would be
lost or overlooked. The reflection upon or interpretation
of the accomplishment of Jesus would be considered by
later hearers to be an end in itself and would no longer
be recognized as simply a later way of representing the
accomplishment but now in language which tends to
obscure. If this should be the case, later Christians
would be interpreting an interpretation with no thought
for the accomplishment; that is, additional reflection
would not begin each time with the accomplishment
itself.

We saw a starting point for this development in the
way in which some accounts in the Gospels have been
placed in secondary historical contexts. In meeting Jesus

men experienced the working of God, and their reflection upon this led to the description of Jesus as the Son of God. Elements such as baptism and the birth accounts in the Christ-kerygma support this. By their arrangement in the Gospels later (confessional) interpretations assume the status of firsthand statements (of what happened), and reflection is consequently divorced from the accomplishment. But these reflections, now isolated from the accomplishment, become the base for still more interpretations, and these later ones, completely divorced from the accomplishment, almost by necessity diverge from one another and lead to the later christological controversies.

As a second possibility, however, the reflection can always be redirected anew to the accomplishment. One then sees that the descriptive words about Jesus or his cross or his coming are cryptic statements which do not in themselves contain the essence of the matter. Their intention rather was to keep alive the thought of what took place in the accomplishment of Jesus by means of descriptive statements about his person or by the interpretation of specific events of his life. The task then is to pierce through these somewhat veiled statements in view of the possibility of a new accomplishment which occurs in preaching.

Consider the sentence: "Jesus is God's Son." Its purpose is not to draw the hearer into contemplation about the kind of person Jesus was, but to make possible the occurrence of a new accomplishment by Jesus. Through him, that is, through the Jesus of the Jesus-kerygma, the work of God is once more set in motion for the hearer.

In a similar way the sentence, "The cross of Jesus is the salvation event" is not meant to provide an objective statement of what happened (historically) on the cross on Golgotha, nor to encourage the hearer to become engrossed with the cross in meditation. Its purpose is to pronounce that Jesus is God's reconciliation for later hearers too.

Through these insights the later, somewhat obscuring interpretations are offset so that the new occurrence of the accomplishment is possible. This is particularly true of eschatological ideas of which later interpretations make good use. These ideas can now be related to the accomplishment, thereby turning the new accomplishment itself into an eschatological event. Understood correctly, preaching is not the announcement that there is an eschatological event, but preaching is itself such an event because it is the continuation of the accomplishment of Jesus.

Consequences

Throughout the history of the church and the history of its dogma these two possibilities have been realized in many different ways. The constant process of reflecting upon and then adding to older interpretations has led to divisions in the church which are still with us today. One group of Christians would adopt one of the later reflections and then label other Christians heretics who supported a different interpretation occurring in another tradition. Divisions were the inevitable result, although they were not due to the evil of men's hearts; they were far more a tragic misfortune, since it was not obvious at the time—and could not be—what kind of reference point underlay each position. But each time later hearers correctly understood the intent of the later interpretations (and penetrated behind their language) a renewal of the working of God, the central issue of Jesus' life, was experienced.

These alternatives merely put the problem in focus. As we have formulated them, they are certainly exaggerated and in their form here false. At all times and throughout the church the reoccurrence of the accomplishment has taken place; and, we may add, the continuing act of interpreting interpretations was never done for its own sake, but for the new accomplishment. That is why it is misleading to draw a sketch like ours.

Nevertheless, I am still of the mind that the problem has to be considered as we have stated it. As Christians reflected further, it was inevitable that earlier levels of interpretation would gradually take on a permanent form. A new accomplishment was not attained every time, nor for that matter were Christians always able to reach back even to the very first interpretations, with the result that these earlier levels became fixed in the course of time. Christians determined, for example, in what sense Jesus was and in what sense he became the Son of God. Perhaps I should say they made their minds up quite firmly about it! As the reflections assumed permanent forms, dogmas evolved from them, becoming, wherever it was possible, obligatory norms of belief for all later Christians! But this development—whether intentional or not—led to a situation in which the accomplishment which Christians did not want to abandon could and should be reached only by working from these later interpretations.

The attitude of the church in rejecting an adoptionist Christology is evidence of this. The position taken was almost unavoidable, since the church reached its orthodox status in areas influenced by Hellenistic thought. It was also understandable that it would be here that emphasis would be placed upon procreation by the Spirit and on the virgin birth.

Despite this, by the end of the second century, during the sixties of the third century, and again around the eighth century adoptionism achieved a relatively influential position. It was no longer an adoptionist Christology directly derived from the Jewish Son of God interpretation, since it had undergone a certain development, although it was somehow still able to hold on to Jewish concepts. It enjoyed the support of theologians of such repute that their names are still known to us today. The controversy over Christology was not decisively settled at the beginning for all generations, as the views of minority parties continued to assert themselves. A result of the sharp dispute with these minorities was, in nearly every case, the excommunication of the theologians (and the groups in the church) who favored an adoptionist Christology.

I do not want to assume the role of a judge in this conflict nor even criticize the church's decisions. Most likely the adoptionists for their part would have condemned their opponents if they had been strong and influential enough (if, for example, they had not been opposed by Charlemagne in the eighth century). Decisions on dogma were indeed all too frequently made with an eye on certain political groups. A discussion about who was really right in those days would be out of place here. It is more important for us to recognize that each side excluded the other from the church by means of mutual excommunication (either actually carried out or planned). Each side made the legitimacy of the accomplishment depend upon the "correct" reflection, and both insisted that the only correct reflection or interpretation (in their opinion) become the criterion for the "church." Anyone holding a different view was a heretic and not a "correct" Christian.

The Interchange of Interpretations

This is the real problem. Both interpretations—the adoptionist Son of God concept of Judaism and the physical Son of God concept of Hellenism—can, if properly used, serve to bring about the accomplishment anew, and do it acceptably. That an individual is able to experience the working of God by placing himself before the kerygma does not depend upon the ideas the interpretation has made use of. Otherwise, as I have shown above, the Christmas kerygma and the Good Friday kerygma could not be brought into any kind of agreement. If these kerygmas are isolated from the points of reference under which they were shaped, contradictions appear, for then the act of reconciliation would have to have occurred either at Christmas or on the cross (or both times). However, no one will dispute the fact that both kerygmas —correctly understood as later interpretations of the accomplishment at two different points in Jesus' life—are able to introduce one to faith. The only reason there has been no serious argument over this is because they have been harmonized by viewing both as part of the salvation event, thereby eliminating the tensions.

The problem of the multiplicity of creedal statements is very similar to the problem of the multiplicity of the major holidays of the church year. A Christmas sermon does not compete with one on Good Friday. It is not clear therefore why a sermon which explains an adoptionist Christology should be considered a rival of one which does the same for a Son of God Christology conceived in physical terms. *The concepts which the reflection has made use of are interchangeable.* If this is admitted (as in the case of Christmas and Good Friday), the problems vanish. But if one dogmatically insists upon specific concepts, then the principle of interchangeability (of such ideas) which is found and practiced in the New Testament is rejected. And the result is schism and splits, both of which are completely unnecessary. They would never have developed in the first place if the purpose of later interpretations with their camouflaging language had been correctly understood. It was not so understood and the continuing practice of interpretation led to division in the church.

It would be anachronistic and thus wrong for us to criticize those conflicts too harshly by blaming (with the help of hindsight) both parties for fixing their attention on the interpretations rather than on the accomplishment. We should admit in all fairness that at the time such methodological insights were still unknown. They were not yet able to differentiate as we can (and must!). But as soon as one has seen that it is the accomplishment that is of central importance and has seen how the interpretations arose and what they stood for, dispute over the concepts and ideas which obscure the accomplishment will cease. To continue the battle today would indeed be anachronistic!

The Problem of Dogma

These concepts and later interpretations cannot and ought not, therefore, be allowed to be the cause of serious divisions in the church today. The body of Roman Catholic dogma I do not really consider to be divisive— in fact I could accept, or at least understand, most of it. But in my opinion it divides the church because it is held in such a dogmatic fashion. Any dogmatizing of interpretations that are products of their time is "exclusive," and therefore divisive. In A.D. 1215 the real presence of Christ in the Lord's Supper was expressed with the help of Aristotelian ideas, as in the teaching of transubstantiation. But it ought not to have been hardened into dogma since we can no longer accept these Aristotelian categories. And even though such a dogmatizing may have been necessary and meaningful then as a defense against false teaching, it should certainly no longer be obligatory today. This objection is leveled not only at Roman Catholic theology but against our church and theology as well —especially against those groups I mentioned at the very beginning of this book, although by no means against them alone.

For us the question of what dogma is is not at all clear. Frequently the very idea is rejected because it is supposedly Roman Catholic. But we still cling to the concept! It is a fact—with or without the concept—that in actual practice there may be several points of doctrine between Protestant and Roman Catholic theology in dispute, but as a whole the difference is merely one of degree: the Roman Catholic church simply has more dogmas than the Protestant church. The Protestant church and Protestant theology are for their part as reluctant as the Roman Catholic church and its theology to see dogmas as obscuring interpretations. The Protestant church is just as loath to concede the principle of the interchangeability of the ideas of these interpretations, and is, consequently, unprepared to recognize new formulations of dogma.

Today we are talking with Roman Catholic Christians more than we did a generation ago, to say nothing of the past four hundred years. But I wonder if we are talking with each other correctly? In our conversations we deal with the symptoms too often without ever actually reaching down to the root of the problem. Occasionally one hears from Roman Catholics that the full Christian truth is not present in the Protestant church; Protestants then reply that the articles of faith of the Roman Catholic church lack the support of Scripture. These arguments completely miss the point. What is defined as Christian truth in the Roman Catholic church is derived from tradition. One need merely think of the history of the development of the dogmas about Mary with one interpretation leading to another in a thoroughly consistent process. But the Protestant church as well takes its idea of Christian truth from tradition, except that it restricts tradition to an earlier period! Does not the difference, then, really have to do with the two attitudes towards tradition, and not with the question of "Scripture or tradition"?

Both churches, resting upon tradition, have used tradition in such a way as to turn interpretations (a part of the tradition) of the accomplishment into dogmas, along with all their ancient concepts. Even Protestant teaching about Christ is not "according to the Scriptures" since it rejects an adoptionist Christology (very much present in the New Testament) and quite one-sidedly clings to post-New Testament decisions on doctrine. That is, we Protestants today cannot be satisfied any longer with the fact that what we call "Christian truth" is found in the New Testament, if we are unprepared to recognize also as "Christian truth" other propositions in the same New Testament. We need to be more accurate in our judgments.

When the catchword "early Catholicism" in the New Testament first appeared, it was greeted with considerable apprehension. Ernst Käsemann stated at the time that the New Testament does not establish the unity of the church, but provides instead the foundation for a variety of creedal confessions. This has not gone unchallenged and should be considered valid only as it suggests that there is indeed a broad base for anyone to find the essence of his creedal statements some place in the New Testament. The question of course is whether the New Testament may ever be used this way. Is it permissible to carefully select statements that support one's position and blatantly ignore those which do not? The New

Testament is the church's oldest extant volume of preaching, as I have tried to point out earlier, and a volume of
preaching cannot serve as a recipe book for dogma. In
fact, it is only when it is used like this that there is any
sense to the argument that the New Testament does not
lay the base for the unity of the church but for a diversity of confessional statements.

We have to admit that the New Testament is often,
indeed, usually, studied in this manner, but the misuse
should be corrected. Käsemann's words could lead to a
certain air of resignation if they were left to stand as is
and if it were not recognized that what is now essential
is a new and completely different reading and use of the
New Testament.

I wonder if a fresh attitude toward the New Testament (by both sides!), as I have tried to establish here,
would not bring about a different utilization of the New
Testament which would demonstrate that, at least to the
degree that it helps restore the unity of the church, it is
the church's book. For if my suggestions are reasonable,
much of what has generally been divisive for the church
becomes ineffective without, however, being eliminated.
Dogmas would then not be understood in such exclusive
terms, and accepting or rejecting them in their present
form or with their ancient concepts would not be a condition of membership in the church or exclusion from it.
Dogmas would be admitted to be interpretations, veiled
interpretations, which are always interchangeable!

It would be quite unrealistic to suppose that one
merely had to say, "Go ahead and do what I have just
proposed and be united." But I would be happy if even

a thin ray of light has been shed, so that thoughts I have offered here—at times strange or even shocking—could be carried out with an ecumenical enthusiasm. They were never intended to undermine or tear down but to help set matters straight and always with the church in mind. The theme "The New Testament as the Church's Book" means therefore that the New Testament, correctly understood, is the book which in all the rich variety of interpretations still produces the one church.

The Question of Truth

The tendencies of the post-New Testament period toward the development of dogma which spawned church divisions as a result of constant reinterpretation are already present in the New Testament. However, the wide assortment of interpretations in the New Testament is no evidence of an already divided church. It is quite true that in the New Testament era there were theological disputes which caused divisions. Paul, for example, would never have admitted that fellowship in the church was possible with gnostic enthusiasts, nor with those still insisting upon the validity of the Jewish law. But it would be difficult to argue that a discontinuity existed between the Pauline churches and the churches of the (later!) pastoral Letters which quite frankly sound different than Paul's letters; they are all part of the same church. It would be just as difficult to speak of a discontinuity because of the not inconsiderable reshaping of the Gospel of Mark by Matthew and Luke for the (later!) churches to whom they were writing.

If the variety of interpretations within the New Testament was never the cause of a single division in the church at the time, then neither should the variety of post-New Testament interpretations as seen in the newly formulated dogmas have been allowed to divide the church. I want to emphasize again that the dogmatizing of a particular idea at a particular time because of the threat posed by false teaching may have been both wise and necessary, provided that the dogmatizing remained true to the accomplishment and expressed it appropriately for the time. But as soon as this temporally conditioned interpretation was given the status of an article of faith, obligatory also for future generations, the freedom of variation of the interpretations was denied, and the dangers we spoke about above came to the surface.

One could object at this point that such a position simplifies the problems much too much. If the contents of dogmas really need not be divisive for the church and if the unity of the church really is a possibility once more simply by giving up dogmatizing as such, would this not mean that what has been called the question of truth is no longer of prime importance? Is tolerance to be practiced at any price and to such an extent that in the end the Christian no longer knows what he is supposed to believe? And would it really still be possible to protect the church against false teaching in a specific instance? Paul's refusal to enter into church fellowship with either the enthusiasts or those maintaining the Jewish law is evidence that there are lines to be drawn (although one may still ask whether there must be such lines simply because Paul drew them). Nevertheless, according to what I have said thus far, there seemed to be genuine harmony. Can we now find criteria by which boundaries can be theologically determined that may not be crossed or cannot be crossed without surrendering the Christian message?

EXISTENTIAL TRUTH

Frequently I have spoken of the new occurrence of the accomplishment of Jesus as the issue of central importance. When the question of truth is raised, the common response is that there can only be one truth, the clear implication being that it must somehow be an objective element capable of being confirmed, established, and formulated. I want to challenge this, for I believe that truth can only be experienced existentially—at least in the theological realm. Obviously, in order to be communicated it has to be put into words, but the process of expressing truth verbally merely stresses its functional character as an address and is at heart different from an objective description.

Faith and Believing

In the discussion between Protestant and Roman Catholic Christians one occasionaly hears, as I have said, the Catholic complaint that Protestants do not possess the complete truth. But is it really necessary to have the "complete truth"? Consider the section on little children in Mark 10:13–16: "Let the children come to me, do not hinder them; for to such belongs the kingdom of God."

When a person is introduced to faith and thereby (as a child or as someone in distress) is placed before God on the basis of this passage, does he still require the preaching of Paul or Pauline terminology? In other words, if it occurs through this Jesus-kerygma (through Jesus!), does he need Paul's views before he is confident that he has been properly and completely introduced to faith? Another example: Shall we say of those who heard only part of the early church's preaching but who still found strength for living and comfort in the hour of death that their faith was incomplete? This would be exactly the case of Paul's mission churches that not only were without the Gospels, but received from Paul practically nothing of the tradition about Jesus which later was incorporated into the Gospels. Furthermore, they would have known nothing of the Deutero-Pauline Letters, the Letters of John, or the catholic Letters. In short, their knowledge of the entire New Testament was frightfully small. Did they therefore have no "complete" faith by which to live and die? Who of us, as a matter of fact, has ever been touched by the whole range of interpretations? Does this mean that our faith is not complete?

Each question, I think, will have to be answered negatively. Faith—genuine, complete faith—is possible, indeed, we must admit, comes to life right where the so-called complete truths of faith are not even known.

The Idea of Faith

I am quite aware that I have been using faith here, or better, *believing*, in a very specific sense. In the study of dogmatics a distinction is made between *fides* quae *creditur* (a faith believed in) and *fides* qua *creditur* (a faith which believes). That is, the difference is between *what* is believed and the execution of faith *with* which one believes. In the first phrase the emphasis is on the object of faith or on the truth to be believed in, and in the second it is on the act of faith reaching after something or some truth. The base of such a distinction is the subject-object relationship. The question to ask here— and not only here but wherever the scheme is suggested —is whether this subject-object arrangement is defensible or of any use. It can, however, still help us to see the issues clearly, if we take it seriously and test it to determine just how far it takes us.

Christian faith is not simply religious belief, a "religious mood of acceptance," or a "vague attitude of openness-for." Neither is it simply an integral part of human existence. It is much more a faith in which some relationship always exists between the one who believes and a definite object of faith. In this sense it is very proper to talk of the subject-object order. It is not possible to allow faith ever to be exercised to its fullest.

But the question is whether it makes any sense at all to speak of the object of faith independently of the exercise of faith, since the *object* of faith is the object of *faith*. When these are separated, the structure is thrown off balance.

Considering the *object* alone has serious consequences for the overall concept of faith, for then we are concerned merely with a *fides historica* (a historical faith, that is, holding facts to be true) and faith becomes little more than a matter of *knowing* things which otherwise cannot be known. On this plane knowledge is drawn from revelation which gives insight into affairs ordinarily inaccessible to me; how else, for example, would I know that Jesus was born of a virgin? But—what effect does such information have on me? Is it relevant for my life and does it make me a new person?

One can object of course that it cannot help but touch me—but, how profoundly? If it is not enough merely to hold something to be true, the implication can only be that, in addition to considering information to be true, I also begin to take it seriously; I allow it to affect the course of my life and through it I become a believer.

Then, however, my act of *believing* comes into the picture again and the question is raised once more whether complete faith exists only where the sum total of all individual truths is present; that is, only where my believing is determined by the *sum of all Christian truths*. If this were the case, it would already have been decided that there can be no actual faith since no one can possibly be influenced by all Christian truths at the same moment. Furthermore, the articles of faith were gradually formulated over a period of time.

It has often been said that truths formulated later were already implicit in earlier statements, only the actual formulations belonging to the later period. This is correct and applies not only to the constantly developing system of dogma of the Roman Catholics but also to what Protestants call teaching or doctrine, such as the pronouncement on the Trinity, for example, which clearly belongs to the post-New Testament era.

But if creedal formulas were already implicit at an earlier stage, then before they were ever formulated, complete faith already existed, and without the necessity of having to *know* the truths of faith—they certainly could not have been known until the creedal statements had been formed. If, however, doctrine B, having developed from doctrine A, was already implicitly contained in doctrine A, then instead of our reckoning with what has been called the truths (plural!) of faith, the issue ultimately focuses on the unfolding of one truth. And, if this is the case, it is incumbent upon the church not to seek differences in these so-called truths of faith, at least not in such a way that later Christians will feel the obligation to retain all of them. It should rather understand the differences as developing from the same point or origin. Faith for me then means that I rest my existence upon the one base, and it becomes truly a complete faith. As one who believes in this sense, I am able to speak of this one point in a number of different ways, always taking care of course to maintain my relationship to it.

The Truth of Faith

This reminds us again that the differing explanations are to be viewed as (partially obscuring) interpretations of this one point. As such, by trying to inform me about and give me access to this original point, they can be extremely meaningful. But it also means that new formulations are always to be sought.

Earlier when I discussed the relationship between Jesus and the activity of God, I attempted to show what the chief interest was in the older apostolic traditions about Jesus with their implicit Christologies. As we made clear the purpose of later interpretations which led to an explicit Christology, there was no thought of separating this explicit Christology from the significant acts and words of Jesus which the christological expressions attempted to illuminate. For this reason I emphasized repeatedly that the predicates ascribed to Jesus are only legitimate to the degree that they express what was expressed in Jesus' life. If now the obscurities of the interpretations are removed—in preaching—so that there is a new experience of God, the main concern must again be what the oldest tradition about Jesus bore witness to. And if I express this as an interpretation, my historical conclusion that Jesus sets God's work in motion will assume the character of an explicit Christology but in concepts quite different from traditional ones. If my historical conclusion is a *truth* of faith, it becomes a truth of *faith* through that preaching which speaks to me.

If I agree with the Christian church in saying that Jesus has risen and then explain this so as to convey the thought that he did not remain in the grave, but left it and ascended to God, this is primarily only a *truth* of faith consisting of facts which I can adjudge to be valid. We are aware of how these statements come about, and I can repeat them as a *truth* of faith—without regard to any original reference point. However, it will not become a truth of *faith* until the proposition affects my existence, and it can only touch me when the same concern becomes important to me as what was (or should have been) important in that statement or article of faith. This can only mean to us now—and should have meant to Christians then—that the one who was crucified was not left in the bonds of death, that the purpose and accomplishment of his life did not come to naught on Good Friday. If I today involve myself with him and his main interest, it is with one who was resurrected, who is living and not dead. Jesus' vital concern was the setting in motion of the working of God. When I experience God's working today through involvement with this same concern as it is proclaimed to me, the resurrection of Jesus becomes for me a truth of *faith*.

The *truth* of faith becomes a truth of *faith* for me as I meet God through Jesus, and I am able to describe the event anew in my own words without being bound to any creedal formula of the past. The older expression may have been transmitted to me in the form "Jesus is resurrected" but now, recognizing that that traditional form is a product of its time, I can speak of the new working of God in the preaching following Good Friday.

As articles of faith both expressions (the old and the new) are different in content and hardly capable of harmonization, but as truths of *faith* they both produce the same results if one works backward from the obscuring effect of interpretation.

The Object of Faith

We saw that we cannot completely dismiss the subject-object relationship, since faith in general can be described as something belonging to human existence, although this is not Christian faith. Christian faith always implies "believing in . . ." and is not merely religious belief. It remains Christian faith through the ages only if what follows the phrase "I believe in . . ." is always the same. The church must always be sure of this. The question, however, is whether this "object" can ever really be expressed.

It is very clear that the interpretations in the New Testament—as confessions of faith—are existential in nature. I can quite easily discover how the object of faith with which we are now concerned was formulated and expressed earlier. There are texts for this which I can exegete.

How are we to define exegesis is a much debated question. It is usually considered to be the whole complex process of understanding by which the issues are brought directly before the modern reader; that is, it is the process of overcoming the temporal and cultural gap and of making the message contemporary for each new generation. This is not without the danger, however, that the reader will fail to differentiate carefully between the individual steps in the long procedure. For this reason I have suggested and already pointed out here that exegesis should be understood only as the first step of the process. Its exclusive concern is always with the past and not with any contemporary message. Contemporary relevance is achieved by translating the ancient message into the modern situation in close association with exegesis as the controlling agent. But exegesis itself is the process of repeating in my language what an author (of a text before me) wanted to say to his reader (in his day).

I have before me the texts by which I want to determine how the object of faith, our present concern, was formulated earlier—in the New Testament. If I now exegete them, I will end up with no more than an understanding of the ideas used by the author of a given text to express the object of faith for the readers of his day. And these ideas are not to be taken as absolute.

It is very important that we do not apply the results of exegesis improperly. It would be incorrect if, in considering these statements of faith for which I must *distinguish* between subject and object, I actually *separated* them and excluded the original subject and—because I now alone consider the object— set myself as the subject in direct relationship with that object. This would indicate that I am not taking seriously the fact that for the authors of these texts the *truths* of faith were truths of *faith;* I would not be taking seriously the fact that these are existential statements.

In the formulation of an existential statement there is always a subjective element. The subjective element is also at the heart of the formulation of truths of faith. I cannot overlook the fact that these truths of faith were formulated by men of a particular time who expressed them in *their* language and with the help of the ideas of *their* culture. This is why the statements of the New Testament period cannot possibly be harmonized so that the objects (the *truths* of faith) toward which faith is directed and which inspire faith are all (with regard to concepts and ideas) described in the same light.

This brings us to the crucial point of the problem. If it is shortsighted to give up the subject-object relationship or if the object cannot be separated and isolated from the older existential statements of faith, then one can speak of this object only as some kind of limit. And this limit is Jesus, not certainly as we find him described, but as the one who (in many different ways) unleashed the work of God for the witnesses of that day and to whom, as such, witness was borne (also in many different ways) by them.

Whoever demands more than this runs the danger of wrongly objectifying existential statements. On the other hand, if we were to abandon talk of an *object* of faith, we would also abandon the *extra nos* of Christian faith (the base outside of ourselves in which Christian faith is grounded). This *object* of faith first becomes the object in the confession of faith of the witnesses, but the confession has all the character of a response that has been prompted by one who in the fullness of his encounter with man has introduced man to faith—namely, Jesus. Only the direct eyewitnesses were present with the earthly Jesus, and since the first Good Friday this relationship could not be repeated. Nevertheless, ever since the first Easter an encounter with the Jesus to whom witness is borne in the church's kerygma has indeed been possible, although that witness gives us a picture of Jesus that is colored by eschatological tones. The description of Jesus with the help of the language and the ideas of that day is the *truth* of faith which in preaching is offered as the truth of *faith*. After Easter, Christian faith has to be considered as a believing *with* those eyewitnesses who experienced the presence of God in Jesus of Nazareth. In believing *with* them, the *extra nos* is preserved. Believing the truth of *faith* of those witnesses does not, however, require later generations to repeat the *truth* of faith in a literal sense. As a matter of fact, variation at this point is not only possible, but quite necessary if we want to make the *truths* of faith understandable; they have to be expressed in new languages and with the aid of new concepts. This necessity, however, does not mean that the concepts can be arbitrarily interchanged, since the newly formulated *truths* of faith as truths of *faith* must always remain faithful to the direct witnesses. Each modern concept must show that it fulfills this function for its own age. Only then does it retain its orientation on Jesus.

The New Testament as the Church's Book

We are now back to the question of the criterion for a theological determination of boundaries we should not cross if we are to remain true to the Christian faith. We have already asked whether the interchanging of interpretations—as suggested earlier—would not yield a situation in which it would be impossible in the end to ascertain where the limits shade off into heresy. But Paul, as we saw, did indeed set himself apart from "Christians" still insisting upon the law. He was correct in this because clinging to the law rules out a proper attitude toward Jesus. In the same way he set himself apart from fanatics who as "Christians" directed their allegiance toward a Spirit-Christ but expressly avoided Jesus.

This answers our question. The criterion—even for contemporary preaching—is the apostolic witness to Jesus as the norm. If a Christian today believes in the *church,* that can be a legitimate expression of Christian faith, but only if he can and does show that it is the same as believing in Jesus. In the same way, believing in the *Bible* can be a legitimate expression of Christian faith, but again, only if it can be and actually is shown how the Bible leads to Jesus. The *truths* of faith in both cases are expressed differently. To treat them as objective elements would mean they would usurp the position of Jesus, and then the boundaries leading to heresy would indeed be crossed. But when these *truths* of faith as truths of *faith* lead us to believe as the first witnesses believed, then the variations of expressions of the objects of faith are of no consequence because they are all interchangeable.

The New Testament is the church's book. But it is the church's book only if it does not stand in Jesus' place. It contains a wealth of statements on Christian faith occurring in a variety of forms. If my preoccupation is with these statements, then the New Testament assumes the position reserved for Jesus. But if I ask where in these *truths* of faith the truths of *faith* are found which invite me to believe as the first witnesses believed, then the New Testament leads me into the faith in which Jesus has placed me.

When it is used in this way, the New Testament also creates the church; perhaps it can even help to bring about the unity of the one church. When it is used in this way, it remains the legitimate point of reference for the church throughout the changing ages.